5
Core
Methods
of
Innovation

by
Sanjeev Sharma

This book is dedicated to my parents
and my family.

PREFACE

I have met many people who want to become successful entrepreneurs and feel that they have the skills and perhaps resources to start a new product based venture. However, they do not know what type of venture they should start and how to identify if their venture would be successful. I realized that while most entrepreneurs are in love with just one idea, there are numerous others who would like to utilize a systematic approach to innovation to create new products. While working in finance, venture capital and technology companies, I had come across many new product ideas and met numerous entrepreneurs and felt that the art of innovation is not well understood and not much material is available to teach this art in a systematic manner. For many years, I have been studying the patterns of consumer needs and solutions in various products and processes. I have identified the core methods of innovation, which I have tried to explain in this book.

INDEX

1

INTRODUCTION

. . . .

In the year 1286 in Italy, Giordano da Pisa invented eye glasses by utilizing convex glasses to correct vision problems. However, it took more than 400 years before a British optician Edward Scarlett created a modern pair of glasses by connecting the frame to a "temple" passing over the ears to hold it. For nearly 20 generations, people had to hold the glass frames in their hands while reading, before this easier way was found. Almost till recently, there has been very little published work teaching various processes to do innovation and due to the absence of such material, it used to take a very long time, before new products could be created with the available technologies.

In the last few decades, due to rapid communication, technology and globalization; rapid innovation has become important to remain competitive for most corporations and Industries. The knowledge gap between nations has been greatly reduced by the internet. While Spaniards could keep the recipe of making chocolate a secret for a hundred years, it is difficult to do so in this small world. With globalization, protectionist trade barriers which used to protect local industries have also been removed by most nations. Leaders, from both the political and business worlds, and from both the developed and developing worlds, have realized that only innovation can give them competitive advantage and have been urging their people to think innovatively.

Political and business leaders in United States and other developed nations have been supporting the off-shoring of jobs hoping that their people are innovative and would create new products and services. Their assumption that future innovation will happen mostly in United States or other developed countries is based on the fact that previously most new products and services were created in the developed world and the developed world has been blessed with the right social, legal and industrial environment to support innovation. However, with the knowledge gap between the developed and developing world evaporating due to the internet and globalization, Innovation has become possible in almost any part of the world. The developing world which till now has been mostly using concepts and products created and tested in the developed world, now has the potential and the capacity to create new products and services on their own.

Just like the last fifty years have produced a breathtaking number of innovations like the Internet, GPS Systems and Mobile Phones and has handsomely rewarded those who have produced innovative products, the next fifty years will also witness a race among nations, corporations and individuals to innovate. This book is an effort to answer two main questions in this space:

1. What are the major ways of doing innovation?

&

2. If a particular innovation would sell in the market?

Do we need inborn skills for Innovation?

For a long time in history, it had been assumed that only a few people with exceptional education and skills can be innovative. It was assumed that Innovation is an inborn talent and only a few people have this skill. When we thought about innovative persons, we started thinking of only people like Thomas Edison, Bill Gates and recently Steve Jobs.

Innovation can be done in a methodical way and the book will explain the different ways of doing innovation. This book attempts to create and lay down different frameworks for innovation, readers can use these to improve upon their existing products and to create new innovative solutions and products.

The book will start with a description of the frameworks, then list a few products and services, categorizing them into the different frameworks. It will then explain how these frameworks can be applied to develop new products and services. Citing examples, it will later test the understanding of innovation examples. The reader will progressively learn to identify different patterns of innovation in various products and subsequently will be able to utilize these frameworks to design new products.

The book will also make an effort to explain how to understand the consumer psychology and find out what new products would the consumer be interested in. Understanding consumer psychology will help in designing of new products. (Based on the author's experience in the venture capital industry, there is a chapter on the venture capital industry which is supposed to play an important role in development of companies with new innovative products.)

Fundamental Research vs Innovation

Innovation is a skill to improve an existing product/service or create a new product or service. The skill of innovation is different from the skills required for fundamental research in science. It requires deep understanding of the scientific theories and processes in a particular and specialized field of science. Fundamental research is done by those who have spent many years in that field; typically these people have advanced degrees in their fields of science.

Innovation, on the other hand requires a keen eye to comprehend existing and available technologies and utilize them to solve particular needs of consumers. Many times, the outputs of fundamental research are utilized by innovative thinking people to create customer-centric products. For example, the founders of Google did research in data mining on internet and used that research to create the Google search engine, which led to many other products from the company utilizing this unique ability. Similarly, fundamental research created electricity which has been used in millions of ways to create new types of products.

Perhaps the ability to identify a customer requirement is more useful than an in-depth knowledge of a particular technology or tool to create a new product or service.

The 3 Categories of Contributors:

The expertise and skills required to do fundamental research are somewhat different from those required to utilize that research to create consumer products. When we think about these two approaches and the important innovators in history, few people have been able to do both the fundamental research as well as utilize that research to bring a product fulfilling customer needs in the market.

Based on the nature of contribution in the process of product development, one can divide the contributors into three categories: Fundamental Research based Scientists, Pure Innovators and those who have been doing both Research as well as utilizing that Research to innovate.

The Researcher / Scientist:

Scientists have been doing fundamental research facilitating new discoveries and evolution of scientific concepts. These contributors have expertise in their field of science and their research produces the basic building block to be utilized in creating new products. The work of these scientists was utilized by many people and corporations to come up with new products and solutions, thus creating wealth for companies, society and nations.

Dennis Ritchie:

Most modern software commercial applications in large organizations are run either on Mainframe machines or on UNIX operating system based mini-computers. Unix is an open source operating system and runs on multitude of cheaper hardware options. Further, most of the software like Database engines, Application Servers, Web Servers etc are written using the C language, another open source language available for free. C language is the base for later languages like C++ and Java. It will not be an overstatement that C and Unix were major contributors to the IT Industry's boom in United States from mid-1980s to 1990s. Denis Ritchie was an American Scientist who created the C Language and was the co-contributor in the development of the UNIX operating system. There are many IT and Internet dot com based billionaires whose innovations were not possible without the C language and the Unix operating system. However, being a core scientist, Mr Ritchie could never utilize his path-breaking creations to get the monetary returns or the fame he deserved. When he died in 2011 around the same time as Steve Jobs of Apple, the media did not pay as much attention to the news of his death. On the other hand, Steve Jobs was the focus of media attention for many months after his death. Steve jobs was not a scientist, nor had he created any path-breaking scientific research, but he innovated to create products that utilized the research done by scientists.

Similarly, Vint Cerf and Bob Kahn, who pioneered the concept of linking computers for National Defense (DARPA), are widely considered as the fathers of the Internet. Being the pure researchers, they did not utilize the power of this work to earn the money they deserved. The power of their work was utilized by others who created multi-billion dollar commercial applications like AOL, Yahoo, Google, Facebook, Amazon.com etc.

The Innovator:

These individuals utilize their understanding of consumer needs and utilize available research work to create new products and services.

Steve Jobs became a billionaire by understanding the needs of the end-user and created desirable products from existing set of technologies. Steve jobs utilized the concept of digital music on a handheld device to create iPod. He later, utilized the concept of smartphones and multi-touch screens to create iPhone. He also created the iPad that supported basic customer requirements from a personal computer and made it easy to use.

Mark Zuckerburg, another innovator has utilized the concept of social networking to create a multibillion dollar company facebook.com. He utilized existing set of available tools on the internet to create this website and made it popular.

Researcher cum Innovator:

A skill to identify a customer need and then how it can be fulfilled by utilizing existing set of technologies is what is required by organizations. Few people have both the skills of doing basic research as well as doing innovation.

One of those few people was Thomas Edison as he was equally successful in doing both the fundamental research on electricity (had over 1000 patents) and using that research to come up with innovative products and selling them. It is noteworthy that many of the companies started by Edison still exist in one or the other form as large profit making corporations. His Edison General Electric which later merged with another organization became GE (General Electric).

In today's world, Larry Page and Sergey Brin, the founders of Google have displayed the capacity of doing both the fundamental research as well as the ability to utilize that research for creating innovative products. The company was founded based on their research work for their PhD program on data mining of the web pages. Their research was utilized to create Google's powerful internet based search engine. Once this fundamental capability of web search was built, other products of Google were created by innovation. For example, Google utilizes data mining about an online user's interests (based on the user's searches, the web sites he browsed and based on the email contents he read) and matches the user to display only those online advertisements that would be of interest to the user.

2

THE FRAMEWORKS
(Innovation Methods)

· ·

ADDITION FRAMEWORK:

The easiest way to innovate is to modify an existing product by adding a feature to it. This is faster than creating a totally new product. The modified new product could be different in many ways. The product could be better in utility, efficiency, ease of use, number of features or appearance. These changes would make the product appealing to the customers, but would not make a totally different product.

Almost all the major consumer products ranging from cars to cellular phones utilize addition framework to come up with newer versions every few years. This is done to keep alive the interest of the existing set of customers, or to appeal to a new segment of customers. For example a Honda's Accord model has multiple versions LX, VX and V6 and the number of features in each have been increasing year after year. Ditto for a product like Apple's iPhone, which has 3G, 3GS, 4G and 4GS versions. The basic functionality of the product remains the same, but addition of new features adds to the appeal and keeps the product in the news.

Addition for Utility:

An example of the "Addition Framework" to increase the utility of a product will be adding a digital camera to a cellular phone to enhance its utility. It makes it appealing to a customer segment who would like the ability of taking digital pictures at any time. In fact, the cellular phones of 4G generation are now carrying 2 cameras, one in the back for taking pictures, and another one in the front is utilized for video-conferencing. A pre-digital age example of addition framework is a swish knife where multiple tools like can openers and screwdrivers have been added to a knife in single product. Similarly, till a few years back, a carbon monoxide detector and a smoke alarm were different instruments used for fire safety in American homes. However later, the carbon monoxide got added to the smoke detector, thus increasing the utility of this product.

Modern electronics and software products can increase the number of features rapidly. The addition framework is being utilized to increase the number of features in many electronics and this can be observed if you look at the cellular phones from a decade ago and compare it with the features of modern phones like iPhone. The modern phones have speaker phones, FM Radio, alarm clock, GPS based navigation system, internet access, and even an operating system. This operating system can be further used to install games, and other software products, making the use of phone virtually limitless.

(The picture above shows the addition of an eraser to a pencil, to increase its utility)

Addition for Efficiency:

An electricity based power or motor is added to many equipments to increase the performance, capacity and usefulness.

Carbon Monoxide is a hazardous gas which can get generated from a mechanical problem in the heating systems or the water heating systems.

The addition framework has been utilized for enhancing efficacy of the Carbon Monoxide alarm. Households in United States have been using the Carbon Monoxide alarms for a very long time. These were mainly battery operated, and as the battery could lose its charge after some time and the Carbon Monoxide alarm could become dysfunctional, which could pose a hazardous situation in case of carbon monoxide getting released from the heating equipments. The newer Carbon Monoxide alarms have added an electric power based operation besides the battery based operation. This addition of power operation has increased the safety feature of the alarm as it can operate in both the situations of either the battery losing its charge or the electric power not being available.

Addition for Appearance:

The packaging industry in United States has mastered the art of improving the appearance of products by addition framework. They have designed attractive packages for almost every product to entice customers. Even fruits like bananas and apples that do not need packaging have a quality sticker on them to impress upon the customers. Similarly, automobile industry has been adding many features every year in car models for increasing the visual appeal and appearance. Honda added the sliding doors in its second generation Odyssey model starting from 1999 where the middle door opens like elevator doors and have sensors to stop if an object comes in the path. Many higher end cars have added front doors which open up towards the sky to add to the visual appeal. In some of its models, Nissan added very expensive Bose speakers and music system, to add to the listening experience of passengers. Similarly, many appealing designs of convertible tops have been added to some cars.

Addition for Ergonomics:

Ease of using a particular product makes it more appealing. Cardboard boxes, especially for large TVs used to be difficult to carry. However, the newer cardboard boxes, have a special cut on the two sides using which two people can carry the box each holding it on one side of it. Similarly, many shirts have a small loop on the inside near the collar. This loop is useful to hang the shirt almost anywhere with no need of a hanger. Another example of addition framework for ergonomics is the addition of heated Seats for comfort of passengers in Cars.

(picture of a shirt loop, makes it easy to hang it almost anywhere)

Addition for safety:

I will give an example of an everyday product to explain about using the addition framework for increasing the safety of a product. Most Americans use the Ironing board, while ironing their clothes. These have been in use for decades now. However, when I purchased a recent Ironing board, I saw an addition of a Hot-Iron holder. The designer of this ironing board perhaps noticed that it is unsafe to keep the hot Iron standing on it (as in the picture one), specially in a house with small children. The holder helps in placing the iron safely.

(While it is obvious that in this first picture, the hot iron is unsafely kept, especially in a house with little children, the second picture depicts that it is much safer in the holder for the iron)

The Process of applying the framework:

Before we explore other frameworks of innovation, we will discuss how to decide what type of addition should be done to a particular product?

To answer this question, a methodical and step by step approach is explained here. Though this process is for the addition framework, it can be applied to other frameworks also:

Existing Features of the Product:

First, the reader needs to identify and write down what are the existing features of the product. It could be the color, size, sound, energy efficiency, ease of use, the utilization of the product and other attributes.

13

The Utility Of the Product:

The reader needs to first identify where the product is currently being used. Is it being used in a specific situation ? in a particular industry ? in a particular geography or country or in a particular weather? The Innovator then needs to understand and see if changes can be made to the product to make it usable elsewhere in other geographies or industries.

Ergonomics:

The reader needs to ask:

1. How the product can be made "easy to use"?

2. Is there any difficulty in using the product either in an obvious or in a non-obvious way?

After identifying the difficulty, the reader should find out how to improve the product by making it more "user-friendly". For example the electronic calculators were initially very small and truly 'pocket-sized'. They were good to carry but were designed to be used only occasionally. However, the small size of both the keyboard as well as the screen was a handicap for people using it for their professions on a daily basis. Therefore, larger size electronic calculators became popular, particularly in the corporate world.

Piggy Bank with an electronic calculator calculating the deposits:

The concept of an age old piggy bank or coin storing jar has been modified recently with an electronic sensor which counts and retains in memory the amount of money which has been deposited in the bank as coins. The addition methodology of innovation is utilized to create this product.

As you insert coins into the piggy bank, the piggy bank's
electronic display shows the total money
deposited in the piggy bank:

Innovating To Make Products Cost Effective:

The innovator needs to understand what adds to the cost of making this product, and then explore a way to reduce these costs. This framework is generally not used for addition framework but primarily used for the subtraction framework, which will be explained later in the book.

How The Product Can Be Made More Efficient To Save Time:

The innovator needs to note down the time the product takes to complete the task it needs to do. Then, the innovator needs to understand the breakup of the sequences and how much time each step takes. He needs to understand if there is a way the product can be modified so that it takes lesser time for the same work. Besides efficiency, the innovator also needs to pay attention to quality.

The innovator needs to check if enhancing the speed has led to any compromise on the quality of results produced. If a change makes the product faster, it might create a lesser quality work and it may or may not be acceptable to customers. The innovator needs to explore if some of the steps in the sequence can be altogether removed from the process. This process is used primarily by the Alternate Means Methodology Framework.

Is the product a status symbol to own now?

Many products like watches and cars are sold as both utility products as well as to display the status of the owners. There is an element of prestige attached to some of these products. The innovator needs to identify what customer segments desire the product in the current form. Is it the professionals, the businessmen, doctors, people in media industry? The Innovator then needs to think how / what can make a larger percentage of this customer segment more interested in purchasing the product.

On the other hand, if the product is a utility product, it could be changed to a status symbol product by utilizing better materials and improving the quality, which would also increase the cost. This has been done in almost all consumer products ranging from clothes to suitcases to watches. The Innovator may benefit by conducting a survey and exploring how desirable the product would be to another segment of customers, after making the changes.

What is the existing usable life of the product.

The Gillette shaving blades have shown immense improvement in quality in the last two decades. While the blades of the late 1980s used to work for a couple of days, some of the shaving blades of today can work for a month. Though these are priced much higher, customers are willing to pay the higher price for these blades.

The innovator needs to ask if he can enhance the usable life of a product.

If the answer is yes, then, will the people be willing to pay for the changes? Consumers are aware that a particular product would start depreciating in performance after some time. It could be a few months or a few years based on the product. An increase in the quality of the raw materials used or making some changes to the product might increase the life of the product. If there is a customer segment willing to pay additional money for increased life of the product, this product can be upgraded accordingly.

Is the product utilizing the current trend or mood of the society?

Can we add a 'fad-element' to the product to make it more popular?: Customers are swayed by certain trends in the market.

For example, since the beginning of this century, customers have strong inclination to purchase products labeled as Green Technologies. Any product which utilizes lesser fuel or alternative green fuels attracts customers. People are willing to pay much higher even if the cost does not justify the increased fuel efficiency of the product. hybrid cars in United States are using the technology of battery powered motor in addition to the gasoline powered engine. The cost of a Honda Civic Hybrid is almost double that of gasoline based Honda Civic. If the cost savings on fuel per year are taken along with the additional maintenance cost for the battery based system, it may not make sense for people driving only a few miles a day to invest in this hybrid car. However, a segment of customers is willing to pay extra anyway as they are committed to the cause of green technologies.

Disruptive Innovations: Ask what the product absolutely cannot do?

In the case of car tires, it was unthinkable that the tire's puncture could be repaired automatically. A slime solution is such a product which can repair a car's tire instantly after a puncture is caused, the product is discussed in latter section.

To create products which are not just incremental in their innovation but are disruptive, the question that needs to be posed by the innovator is what is it that would be unthinkable for a product to do, and then later find out ways to accomplish that task. Heating food without fire or heat, by using microwave is another older example of disruptive innovation.

Earphones with Retractable Cords:

The picture here depicts the addition of a retractable cord with earphones. This addition makes the earphones sleek and easy to use, and avoids the inter-twining of the long cord of earphones.

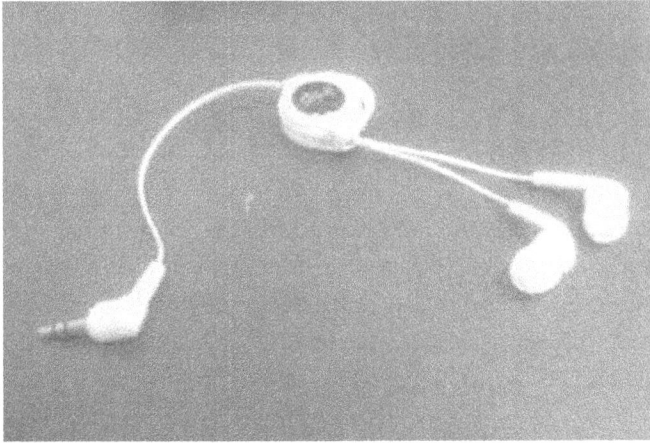

SUBTRACTION FRAMEWORK:

A subtraction based innovation is based on reducing the number of technical features and the amount of material being used in the product.

Many products are designed and manufactured with many add-on features. In some products, many of these features are barely used by the customers. Further, many customers find it too complex to understand so many features in a single device.

Therefore, reducing the add-on features can make the product easier and simpler to use. As an example, in the 1980s, the earlier versions of VCRs had many features like timer based recording features, flying erase head and an alarm clock. These features added to the cost of the product, but the features were hardly used by most customers. Many customers needed the device to simply watch a movie or may be record a TV program once in a while. These customers did not need the additional features and in-fact found it too difficult to understand how to use the additional features. Therefore, the later versions of VCRs did not have these features and were priced much cheaper.

For a subtraction based innovation methodology, the innovator needs to ask the following questions:

What is the main utility of the product and what are the unused additional features?

Besides the main utility of the product, how many of the additional features are actively used by the customers. Which of the features of the product are almost never being utilized by the customers? The innovator can start by removing the less-used features of the product.

What are the cost components of this product ?

Is it possible that we can reduce the cost of the product by reducing the material used, or by using cheaper processes or cheaper components? In the 1990s, a landline based cordless phone sets had many features like a voicemail recording device and a speakerphone. But, now, as people have started using cellular phones as their primary phone and as the voicemail recording feature is provided by the telecom companies, speakerphones and voicemail recording features are not that desirable by customers and are not as popular in cordless phones.

Creating a separate product using a Subtraction Framework?

Sometimes, a product has an important add-on feature but it is rarely used by the customer due to the complexity of using this feature. Many customers are interested only in the main product and do not need this add-on feature. In such a case, the extra features can be removed from the main product to create it as a separate product. This separate product can become popular with a different customer segment due to the ease of using this product.

ALTERNATE MEANS FRAMEWORK:

As the name suggests, this methodology of innovation is based on utilizing an alternate means of attaining the end-goal. The end-goal in this case does not mean the product itself but rather the utility of that product. For example, an electric oven utilizes an alternate means of cooking compared to a gas-burner based oven. Similarly, a microwave heats food using an alternate process of using microwave technology. Similarly, while a candescent bulb used to consume more electricity generating heat than generating light as it was based on heating a filament, a solution was found by a creating a fluorescent bulb, which instead of heating the filament, utilized a mercury vapor that created light when energized. As mercury is considered a health hazard, LED based light bulbs have now started becoming popular. These Light Emitting Diodes based lamps have multiple LEDs in one lamp, these have higher efficiency in terms of converting electricity to light and have longer life.

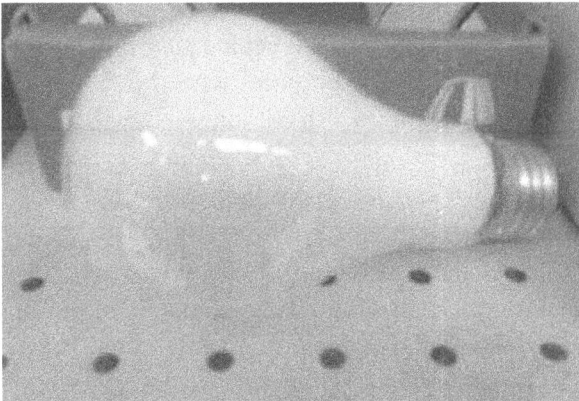

(Picture of an LED bulb on sale above)

Writing Instruments:

While a Fountain Pen was used traditionally for writing, it had various issues: It had to be re-filled in short intervals, and sometimes on almost a daily basis. Further, it could leak and its nib point would bend regularly, which had to be replaced. A ball point pen utilized a thick refill, which would neither leak, nor would it require to be replaced on a daily basis. The nib of ball point pen was strong and would not bend or become useless by merely falling on the floor. A pencil does the same job as a writing instrument, and since it can be erased easily, makes it useful for certain tasks like drawings and designing. While traditional pencils needed a pencil sharpener (also called parer in UK), a refillable mechanical pencil was created which had a "lead" based refill, that could be changed in the mechanical pencil holder made up of plastic or metal. Later, many alternate forms of Pens satisfying the writing needs of customer have been created

For the alternate means methodology, the innovator needs to identify what is the main purpose of the end-product. He then needs to search for the alternate technologies which can be utilized to create / perform the same task or a similar task which may be acceptable to customer. The innovator would then need to find a match between these technologies to create a new product.

The following questions need to be asked in this methodology:

- What is the main goal of using a particular product?
- Are there alternate technologies available which can be utilized to create a product serving the same purpose?

If there are many technologies available, the innovator needs to understand what would solve the customer's major complaints with the existing product. Even if the customer is satisfied with the existing product, the customer may start using the newly created product in many situations. For example a gas-based oven is preferred by most customers, but in some locations where gas is not supplied by utility companies, an electric based oven is utilized.

Sometimes, a completely new type of a product creates its own market, after it is launched, for example, before a microwave was launched, customers did not desire it, but later its use created demand in the market. A similar case is that of an iPod, An iPod is an alternate means of storing and listening to songs, compared to previous products like CD-Players or Walkman which utilized compact disks and tapes. Such products may be called lifestyle products as they were not needed or desired by customers before they were introduced in the market.

Similarly, a large variety of mattresses, like box-spring based, foam based and air-filled ones are examples of alternate means methodology of innovation: each type of mattress has slightly different advantage and use over the others.

Door-top hanger:

For a long time, people used to insert nails into the "inside" side of wooden doors to hang their clothes. It was messy and not sleek.

Plastic and metal based over-the-top hangers were designed that served the purpose of hanging clothes in a sleek way.

Steel Flasks:

The previous generation '*Thermos*' or flasks had a glass shell inside them. However, these glass shells used to break very quickly if the flask fell down. Newer flasks were designed with steel interiors and a vacuum between the outer and inner steel surfaces. These are now popular as they are more durable and perform equally well.

COMBINATION FRAMEWORK:

A Combination Methodology is an advanced methodology to satisfy a challenging customer need. In this methodology, first a need is identified, then in order to create a product to satisfy this need, different technologies are combined together to create a new product. This methodology is very powerful and results in breakthrough products. However, it requires that the innovator should be able to scan a large number of available technologies and identify the ones which are relevant. Combining different technologies to create a new product requires support of the experts in each of the different technologies which are being combined.

The Combination Methodology requires that first a detailed process flow with individual steps is created for the goal. Then, for each of the individual steps, available technologies need to be identified. Finally, different combinations of these technologies or processes are studied and the optimum ones are chosen by the innovator.

e.g.

Bomb detection instrument using bees:

Scientists were struggling to find a way to detect bombs in airports and other transportation hubs.

One way was to train dogs, however it costs a lot of time and effort to train the dogs. Scientists realized that bees are equally good at sniffing smells. They trained bees to signal particular smells. Then inserted these bees in a closed container where the movement of these bees' antennas were being monitored by cameras. Cameras would raise alarm on noticing the movement of antennas of these bees, which would alert the security officers about the detection of bombs by the bees. More details of this device are explained in the later chapter 5 of Examples.

Super fast airplanes:

There has been research going on to create an ultra-fast aircraft. One of the designs that has created lot of excitement promises to fly from US to Japan in 30 minutes. This design utilizes combining the Rocket technology with the technology of the airplane.

Kindle:

An electronic reading device made by combining the concept of a magnetic writing pad and an electronics based storage. The age old children's writing pad had a magnetic pen which would be used to write in black color on a white screen, but would be erased easily. The advantage of this resulting device is that there is no light emitting out of the device and you get a paper based reading experience from the device. Though the concept was designed using transposition methodology as will be explained in a later chapter, the product was created using Combination Methodology:

The complexity of implementing a Combination Methodology highlights the importance of local networks in a business, for example the entertainment industry is localized in Los Angles, the automobile industry in Detroit and the finance industry in New York. This is despite the fact that internet and telecom have made it easy for people to work on the same project from different places and there is theoretically no need for industries to be localized. All these industries are constantly innovating new products often utilizing the combination methodology. Having localized expertise helps in the collaboration required for doing innovation. With increasing globalization, when expertise in multiple areas starts getting dissipated to other countries, the power of a nation to innovate alone thins down and it has to rely on the skills available in other nations.

Similarly, corporations which are outsourcing part of their work to outside organizations need to understand if the work being outsourced is of strategic importance to their innovative needs. For example, many of the finance companies in New York have now outsourced software maintenance work to consulting companies based in Asia. Many of these software programs were created with business algorithms unique to the corporations and were providing a competitive edge to the organizations. Once the work is outsourced, the domain knowledge of the algorithms also gets shared with outside consulting organizations over a period of time. Further, any change to these algorithms becomes challenging for the decision makers owing to the domain knowledge expertise being in a different country and time zone. Further, the change in the algorithm is no more "within" the company, as it is being done by an outside consulting organization. Over a period of time, the organizations lose their competitive edge over other organizations in the industry.

TRANSPOSITION FRAMEWORK:

When airplanes were being designed by observing how a bird is able to fly in the air, they were using transposition methodology of innovation.

Transposition in innovation is perhaps the most advanced methodology for designing a new product. I used the word "design" and not "create" here, as this methodology will help in visualizing a new product. You may need to use any of the previously discussed methodologies to create a prototype of the product.

Transposition requires understanding one or a few attributes from one product and applying those to another product, to create a substantially different product. Then, the methodology requires the innovator to go deeper into the customer psychology and understand which of the many attributes in a product are appreciated by the customer and can be applied to another product to create the same effect.

These attributes could be of a wide variety: the size, color, shape, weight, ergonomic features, efficiency, energy consumption, ability to be carried, strength, materials used etc.

One example of transposition is the use of internet based games for teaching management courses. Traditionally, management courses were taught as theoretical concepts. Later, many business schools realized the importance of using case-studies to students. Case-studies were written based on exhaustive studies on a particular business event and were useful to get a complete perspective on a real-life situation. However, in the last few years, it has been realized by many business schools that reading about previous case studies is not as effective as making decisions to solve an active problem. This is important to develop decision making skills. Thus, many software companies have utilized the concept on online games to give management education to students. These games create a mutually competing environment for students where students apply their management concepts to make decisions and win in the game. One of the early successful games is the MARKSTRAT online game, which teaches marketing strategy to management students.

Though any number of products can be created with Transposition Methodology, understanding the needs and desires of the consumer is the key to create a product that will create demand in the market. Therefore, transposition cannot be done in isolation but can only be done by indepth understanding of customer behavior and needs.

Kindle: Transposition of paper book reading to a computer screen.

Let me explain this with a relatively recent product in the market the Kindle e-Reader device from Amazon.com. Amazon.com realized that many people still prefer reading from paper based books compared to reading on a computer screen or a laptop screen. One of the main disadvantages of reading from a computer screen is that there is light emitting out of the computer screen and it shines into the eyes of the reader. After reading from the screen for some time, the eyes get tired much faster than reading from a paper book.

The primary attribute of a paper based book is that it needs an external light source. On the other hand, the primary advantage of a digital book is that there is no additional weight of a digital book on a hard disk and you can carry thousands of digital books in a single computer hard disk. The need was to bring this paper-book type of reading experience where you need an external light source to a computer screen. After searching for available set of technologies, Amazon.com found an e-Ink based grayscale display which it utilized to create this e-Reader. The device gives the feeling of a paper-book as you need an external light source. It does not hurt your eyes like a computer screen and therefore you can read for many hours without feeling tired.

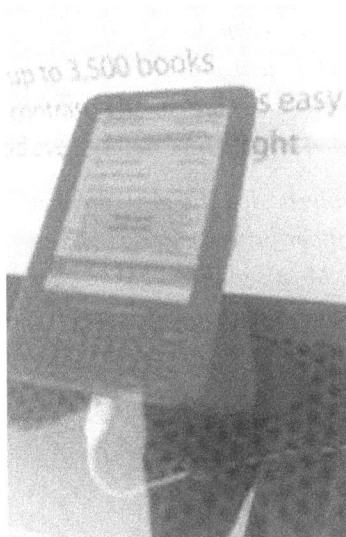

(This picture of kindle displays the e-ink based screen which does not emit any light.)

Transposition of Fiber Optic Communication To A Computer Chip:

Semiconductor chips are the heart of a computer systems. They transfer and compute information using binary code. The concept of binary code is based on signals composed of zeros and ones. Electrons were utilized for these signals using in the electronic components. The main issues were always speed and heat generated in these components. While major chip making organizations like Intel have been coming up with newer designs for more than two decades to increase speed using electrons and reduce the heat generation in the chip, Mr Raj Dutt, CEO of APIC instead used transposition methodology to solve two problems. He took the concept of communication of data over long distance using fiber optic lines in telecommunication industry and applied it on a semiconductor. In this process, since light is utilized to transfer the signals, there is hardly any heat generated and the speed is the fastest.

In the words of Mr Dutt:

"The significance of the technology is that information transfer on the semiconductor chip as well as between components, will now be done using light - photons - instead of just electrons (electronics)," California-based Dutt told PTI.

"Photonic interconnects do not generate heat and use less size than electronic copper interconnects, so more transistors can be put onto a chip. Most significantly, we have figured out how to do this using the same economical process used in manufacturing semiconductor chips today, enabling them to be stamped out by the millions,"

Transposition may result in absurd hybrid products:

Can we use transposition of characteristics from any product to any other product?

It is possible to use transposition from any product to any other product, though the customers may not like the resulting product. Let me explain this by an apparently absurd example:

I am writing this part of the book while travelling by train in the east coast of United States. As I look out of the window of my train, I see an apple tree. Then I look at my laptop computer where I am typing. I wonder for a moment, if transposition can be used as an innovation technique between a tree and a laptop. Let us explore this seemingly absurd idea of using the properties of a Tree to improve the laptop design:

Let us write what are the characteristics of a tree:

1 It grows from the earth

2 It has roots

3 It can give fruits

4 It has green leaves

5 It has a large size

6 It has wooden branches, which can be cut and still the tree continues to live

7 It is quite strong to take the impact of wind and rain and still survive

8 It generates oxygen, and is thus good for environment

The first and second characteristics will be impossible to implement, but the following could be utilized for transposition for my laptop to make it a different and better product:

1 Large size (may be it is better to have a larger laptop for ease of use, rather than just the smaller versions). A larger screen and bigger keyboard could be desirable characteristics.

2 Detachable parts (today's laptops are all compact single units. But, may be the screen, the keyboard, the mouse and the motherboard could be made removable from the unit, probably foldable and kept separately and made able to communicate wirelessly to give much better ergonomics)

3 Sturdiness (Today's laptops are best for use inside the home or outside. But a much better quality laptop could be created which can be safely used outside the home and does not get impacted by sunlight, wind or a little bit of rain).

4 Environmental Friendly:

In order to make the laptop more environmental friendly, let us first look at what is making it less environmental friendly and explore the means to improve those:

- The batteries have to be replaced after some use and the old batteries usually do not get recycled. Ideally, we should utilize batteries of a quality that never needs to be replaced.

- The amount of power consumed by the laptop can be reduced by many different means.

- The amount of heat the laptop is generating should be reduced.

The next step would be to find means and technologies to achieve these goals.

Here is a second and even more absurd example of Transposition Methodology:

Now, vice versa, can we try to Transposition a few traits from a laptop to a tree?

With current advances in biotechnology, we can try to bring in some of the traits from a laptop to an Apple Tree.

The characteristics of a laptop computer are following :

1 It is user friendly

2 It can be used in many different ways by installing new software

3 It can be connected to internet and can be used to monitor other places

4 Thru network technology we can monitor this laptop remotely and see its performance

I can think of making this apple tree a bit more user-friendly - by changing its height and width to make it easier to pluck fruits and also maximize production of the fruit. Perhaps the Apple fruit can be genetically modified to bring in alternate and more nutritional value, if this modified fruit would be useful and desirable by the consumer is a question that requires another debate. The apple tree grows in only certain cold weather conditions, may be it can be modified to grow in warmer weather also.

Therefore, though the innovation possibilities are endless with Transposition Methodology, the innovator needs to understand what is desired by the consumer.

INNOVATION IN PROCESSES:

Since the late 1950s, the world economy, the developed world in particular has been growing primarily on the basis of a robust service sector. During this period many innovations have been utilized in the process space. There were periods when certain types of process innovations became popular. Industries were developed for teaching and certifying new processes. In the 1980s, the concept of TQM (Total Quality Management to make quality a part of every step of manufacturing) became popular. Then, in the 1990s, the ISO series (for quality, procedures and process flows, documentation and security) certifications became popular over Europe and Asia. Many organizations have spent large amounts of money to get their workers trained and get ISO certified, for example ISO 9000 series.

The Japanese popularized the concept of JIT Methodology (Just In Time Methodology) to save on waiting/lag time between different steps of a process. There were interesting stories in the media in 1980s that future ships carrying coal and iron ore from Australia will process these raw materials on-their-way to Japan to be just-in-time ready for the final processing in the Steel Plants. Another process methodology that became popular in the last decade is the Six Sigma which initially started for the manufacturing sector but has now been implemented in the services sector. The Six Sigma process is based on utilizing data to ensure a very high quality of work and minimizes the errors while providing service. The six sigma certification's goal is to reduce the defects to a level of 3.4 defects per million.

Need based innovation in shaking hands during Swine Flu days:

Certain situations force people to use alternate steps for their processes and means. During the summer of 2009, my colleagues and I decided to change the way we shake hands to reduce the probability of catching swine flu. We decided a new way of shaking hands by simply touching each other's elbows slightly thereby avoiding direct contact of palms. When swine flu subsided, we returned to our normal way of shaking hands. Sometimes we wonder if the Swine Flu had not subsided, perhaps this alternate way of acknowledging each other would have become popular !

An innovator creates a new process due to many reasons. Sometimes, it is done due to an obvious need and sometimes it is done to make an existing process more efficient by using a new technology or by changing the sequence of steps. The goal is usually for higher quality and higher efficiency. The innovation Frameworks of Addition, Subtraction, Alternate Means, Combination and Transposition that are applicable to products are also applicable to Processes. A few additional innovations frameworks applicable to processes are:

Assembly Line Process:

When Henry ford invented assembly line for manufacturing automobiles, he was doing a process innovation. He created a detailed step by step breakup of the process of manufacturing an automobile. Instead of manufacturing one vehicle at a time, he created a process where multiple vehicles are produced simultaneously. In this process, parts and material are added optimally to the vehicle-in-construction based on logistics. One advantage of this process is that the skill-set required from workers at each of the steps is very narrow for that step, for example one worker is doing only welding, another one is only attaching the mirrors, a third one is adding seats etc.

Assembly line process makes the skills of manufacturing a vehicle commodity skills. Since each worker's skill set is very narrow, it is easy to replace workers from most of the spots on the assembly line with little training to the new worker taking the spot of the previous one.

Most modern service based Corporations in sectors like banking, finance, information technology and pharmaceuticals have utilized this assembly line process. HR departments call it the Matrix Organization structure versus the previous Hierarchical organization structure. In the hierarchical organization structure, an employee works for a particular manager and the manager gives multiple tasks to this employee to get the work done. There were periods when the employee had little work and there were periods when the employee had too many tasks to be completed all at once. Over time, the employee becomes an important person in the organization as he has domain knowledge of multiple tasks and the process flow of the jobs. This organization structure makes the organization dependent on the services of a person who has spent a few years in a particular organization. The employee would usually get increasing responsibility with every promotion.

In Matrix organizations, all processes are divided into tasks and each task is distinguished based on the skill required to complete this task. Those skills which could be utilized to complete tasks from multiple processes are identified. Then, workers are hired to work only using certain very specific skills and they are supposed to support multiple projects and groups using those skills. Workers in this organization structure do not get work from one manager, but from managers of multiple projects and groups. This process maximizes the utilization of a worker in the corporation. However, for a white collar worker, this process ensures that the worker gets very limited exposure to the larger organization structure and business processes, thus limiting his growth opportunity. This work environment is also mocked as a "cubicle" culture by some people. Due to Information technology, the business process steps have been automated and workers suffer from this organization structure as they are restricted to using a very small subset of their skills and hence get limited growth opportunities.

Standardizing Process:

Standardizing Technique is applied to make a process more efficient and faster. An example of standardizing of processes is the use of shipping containers.

Before the 1950s, goods were shipped to different countries using non-standard containers. These containers were difficult to load and unload at different shipyards. For example it was difficult for different shipyards to handle one thing in a container of 33 feet, another one in a barrel and a third one in a crate. Further, each shipyard had different equipment and capabilities. In the 1950s, the concept of standard 20 feet and 40 feet shipping container was invented by Keith Tantlinger. This revolutionized the speed of shipping and managing the goods as the same standard equipment to handle goods became available at all shipyards and trucks are available across the globe to carry these standard size containers.

As another example of standardizing framework, the QWERTY keyboard is a product used for standardizing the process of typewriting.

PROCESS INNOVATION IN INTERNET COMPANIES:

Internet based businesses are about process innovation. Each of the major internet based companies (like eBay, Amazon, Facebook etc) understood a non-obvious need of consumers and created a unique set of processes to serve that need. These companies consider many of these processes as inventions by them and have filed patents for these processes.

Online Auctions:

eBay realized that online customers and small companies would need a platform to sell and auction their products, both new and used ones. When ebay.com filed patents about its processes of doing internet based Auctions, many people raised eyebrows. There was criticism that the concept of auction exists for a long time and ebay did not invent any original process and therefore should not be allowed to patent the process of internet based Auction. However, eBay defended itself and also protected its patents by aggressively threatening with lawsuits other companies trying to do internet auctions in exactly similar steps. eBay's strategy has been to find the most optimum way of doing online auctions, and get that process patented. Though other companies have started online auctions, their processes follow different set of steps and methods from eBay's.

Similarly, reverse auctions are becoming popular by electronic procurement companies. These are utilized by corporations trying to get online bidding from suppliers and contractors. An example of an emerging economy company in this space is a company eProcurement Technologies Pvt Ltd, based in Ahmedabad, India that has developed an online procurement software. This software enables corporations to get bidding done on its requirements of supplies and contract work. To increase security, it utilizes biometric authentication to authenticate the bidding contractors, suppliers as well as the purchasing corporations' officers.

All-Under-One-Dot-Com Strategy:

Jeff Bezos from Amazon.com understood that a segment of customers would be willing to order books on internet and would be willing to wait for a few days for the book. Amazon.com started with selling books but has now taken the strategy of "all-under-one-dot-com" and is selling a wide range of products and services.

To explain the all-under-one-dot-com strategy, I will site a personal experience. In late 1999, my sister in India needed to purchase a book which was out-of-print for a long time, but was required for her research work in her Master's program. After unsuccessfully searching for the book in New Delhi, she asked me to find the book in USA. I used Amazon.com to make a search but could not find the book. However, Amazon.com sent me an email stating that they have sent a search request to their network of used book resellers. After a week, I got another email from Amazon.com stating that they found the book with one of the used book sellers and gave me a quotation, which was a reasonable price. It was a very pleasing experience and I realized that Amazon.com is on a mission of making sure that the customer does not return without purchasing from its online store. It wanted to sell everything the customer needs through their website. They had decided that no-matter-what, the customer's every need must be satisfied through their website. They want to make it a "Walmart" of internet with everything available under one roof and probably more. Today, Amazon sells almost everything: from sports equipment to software to hardware to music and movies on its website. Further, there are price comparisons between multiple sellers and the consumer does not feel like checking other online stores. Recently, I wanted to purchase a children's left-hand golf set for a girl child as a gift.

After trying at major sports stores, where I could not find it, I tried it at Amazon.com where I was able to find it at a reasonable price. Once again, Amazon.com gave me the same satisfying and pleasant experience which I had first experienced twelve years back.

Social Networking:

The founder of Facebook, Mark Zuckerberg realized that a segment of customers is willing to share the details of their friends and family on internet with others and would be willing to ignore the privacy issues. Facebook has been aiming at harnessing the experience of the online friends of a customer in multiple ways. If a customer is interested to buy a tool, he can utilize the ratings given on the various choices by the customer's online friends. Similarly, linkedin.com utilizes the concept of sharing the contacts with your online friends for mutual benefit. Many companies have jumped to the social networking bandwagon and grow in this segment. Zynga.com has combined the concept on online games and social networking to become the largest social network game web site in the world. In Dec 2011, Zynga did an IPO in US market, which received wide media attention.

Search Engine and Customer Profiling:

Google is quite different from all of these other online companies we discussed. It is different as it is based on proprietary expertise on data mining for finding relevant web pages, which other companies could not do. The business concepts of consumer-to-consumer commerce, business-to-consumer commerce and social networking could be replicated with known technologies, but the search engine technology of Google is proprietary and not available to others. Google also profiles the customer and focuses on using this deep knowledge of customer behavior to sell relevant products and services to the customer.

Privacy vs Profiling Approach:

Numerous companies on internet have started doing profiling of the customers. Companies like Google have expertise in profiling a customer based on the searches, email content and the websites visited. Sometimes, this is helpful to customers when the website can display relevant advertisements. However, many customers consider it an invasion of privacy. The fact that their web searches and email content are being tracked by the internet based company is disliked by many. Customers have started realizing that social networking companies like linkedin and facebook are keeping all their communication and contact details with them, and can make them available to others at a price. It is no surprise that only a small percentage of fortune 500 CEOs are utilizing social networking websites to keep in touch with their contacts.

Therefore, a new customer-segment has emerged that wants complete privacy and safety of their personal contacts and communication and would even be willing to pay for it. Few companies have yet addressed this group of customers.

Customer Centric versus Vendor Centric Approach:

Craigslist.org started as an internet based classifieds website where people could post their requirements anonymously as well could advertise their products and services.

This was useful to many but there was no way to find out if the people advertising their skills were certified, experienced or not.

ServiceMagic.com was started to target those customers who wanted only certified and experienced service providers. However, the business model here was that the customer would have to first post his requirements and the requirements would be displayed to the service providers. Service Providers would then approach the customer with their quotes. In this model, the control of the transaction was more in the hands of the service provider than the customer, as the service provider would be able to see the requirements and respond if he desired to work on the project or had the time.

There was a gap between these two models. Craigslist had both skilled as well as unskilled service-providers available, but it was difficult to determine who had good skill; while servicemagic.com provided access to only certified service providers. Neither of these models were providing access to non-certified handymen who could be trusted by customers for good work. There was a need for a website where customers could find the ratings providing by fellow customers to identify handymen or other service providers. A few websites have recently emerged to provide this need of customers, for example Skillslate.com and Angieslist.com. Here the service providers list their skills and their hourly rates. Further, their ratings given by previous customers are also displayed to customers. This website allows the customer to pick up handymen and service providers who may or may not be certified but have provided good service to previous customers.

Regionalization Approach:

There are many successful clones of larger internet companies focusing on customers of a particular community, country or language. Among the South Asian, a portal Sulekha.com and Rediff.com have become popular for posting classifieds among South Asians. Similar web sites are popular among European and other Asian communities.

Aggregation Approach:

Some websites have become popular as they are able to accumulate information from other websites in one particular site. Samachar.com has news information from multiple websites at one place. Finance.yahoo.com has financial news from different sources at one place. A website seekingalpha.com aggregates financial domain content provided by users.

3

THE 4 STEPS IN AN INNOVATION LIFECYCLE:

. . . .

" *There's more at stake than exported jobs. With some technologies, both scaling and innovation take place overseas. Such is the case with advanced batteries. It has taken years and many false starts, but finally we are about to witness mass- produced electric cars and trucks. They all rely on lithium-ion batteries. What microprocessors are to computing, batteries are to electric vehicles. Unlike with microprocessors, the U.S. share of lithium-ion battery production is tiny.*

That's a problem. A new industry needs an effective ecosystem in which technology knowhow accumulates, experience builds on experience, and close relationships develop between supplier and customer. The U.S. lost its lead in batteries 30 years ago when it stopped making consumer-electronics devices. Whoever made batteries then gained the exposure and relationships needed to learn to supply batteries for the more demanding laptop PC market, and after that, for the even more demanding automobile market. U.S. companies didn't participate in the first phase and consequently weren't in the running for all that followed. I doubt they will ever catch up."

– Andy Grove, Co-founder of Intel in a 2010 article.

Innovation is not a continuous process, but is done in steps. There are four major steps in the innovation lifecycle of a product:

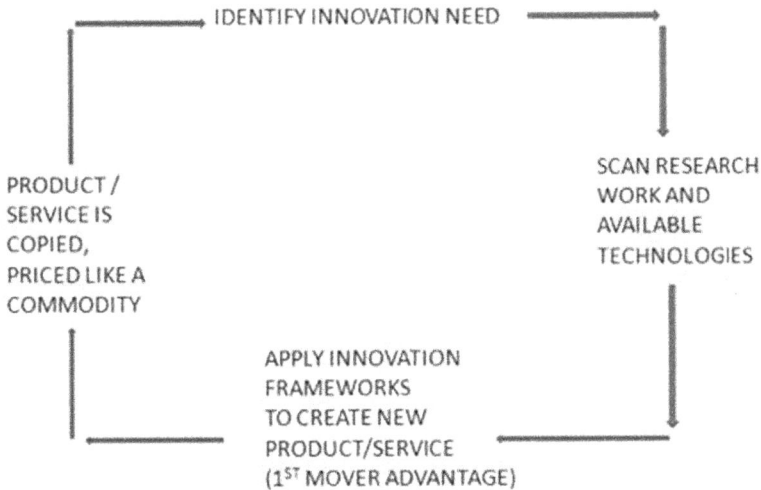

IDENTIFY INNOVATION NEED

SCAN RESEARCH
WORK AND
AVAILABLE
TECHNOLOGIES

PRODUCT /
SERVICE IS
COPIED,
PRICED LIKE A
COMMODITY

APPLY INNOVATION
FRAMEWORKS
TO CREATE NEW
PRODUCT/SERVICE
(1ST MOVER ADVANTAGE)

Step 1: First, an obvious or hidden need of an Industry or customers is identified. This is the time a company starts allocating budget for capital expenditure of R&D. The company identifies an existing product that can be modified to fulfill the demand or starts designing at an altogether new product.

Step 2: Then, a range of new fundamental research materials are scanned that could be utilized. The Research Process is continuing in this period and the skills to identify relevant research work are required to design the new product.

Step 3: Using innovation frameworks described previously like Addition and Transposition, a new product fulfilling the need of the consumer is created and launched. This is the phase where premium pricing can be charged for the product due to the first mover advantage. This is the period where both revenues and profits of the corporation go up.

Step 4: After some time, other companies catch up and create similar products and due to competition, the product price starts falling. In this phase, scale of economy reaches for the production and the cost price also starts falling, but overall there is pressure on the profitability of the product. This is the time when CEOs start thinking how to keep the profitability of the product from going lower.

Again, in order to be competitive, the company realizes it needs to innovate more. It needs to go back to step 1 to identify further ways of enhancing the product by utilizing new research or come up with a new product. However, there is some time lag between the step # 4 and going back to step #1 again. It may take many years of fundamental research before a new technology arrives which could be utilized to go back to step #1 and create a new product.

Unfortunately, many companies do not have the patience at step # 4 to wait for a few years for new usable technology to be created. This is the time when management thinks of increasing the profitability of the organization by cutting costs and one of the easiest ways is outsource the jobs to an outside company or another country where the work could be done cheaper.

The Changing Face of A Television:

It took nearly twenty years for TV Industry to come up with a color TV in 1960s from the Black & White TV of 1940s. Then, it took more than thirty years for the flat screen TVs to arrive in the 1990s. It took nearly another decade of innovation for Plasma and LCD TVs to start becoming popular. And very recently after 2010, the LED TVs have started becoming popular.

The first phase of innovation in TV Industry happened in United States. However, as TV Industry moved out of United States in 1980s, almost all the innovation of flat screen TVs, LCD TVs etc happened outside United States, mostly in Japan.

As Andy Grove has stated, once you outsource the production of a product to another country, all the skills also go away. This makes it difficult for the new wave of innovation to happen in this product within the same country. As the Industry and all associated skills are now in another country, any associated innovation also happens in that country. As explained by Andy Grove's article, if you outsource the work to another country during step number 4, you would have no capacity to go back to step #1 in that Industry.

Perhaps, Business leaders should start identifying the phase 4 of the innovation cycle (when product prices become low due to intense competition) to a phase that requires the use of innovation frameworks to get back into the first mover advantage. However, business leaders need to have patience as there is a time lag between identifying this phase, identifying relevant new technologies and applying the innovation frameworks. The innovators in the organization need to have the skills to identify relevant technologies which can be applied for the innovation lifecycle to continue.

Evolution of the Internet based Telephony:

While Internet started becoming popular in the early 90s, the concept of internet based voice started becoming popular only a decade later, in early 2000s. In the beginning it was voice over internet where both the parties were connected to internet. Many internet based software solutions like Yahoo Messenger became popular during this period. The next phase was transfer of voice calls from Internet to land lines. It utilized a process of converting sound into data to be transferred on the internet for the majority of distance, and then transfer this data from internet back into sound for the land line at the last leg of travel. This still required sitting in front of a personal computer and being logged into an internet based software service like Yahoo messenger to make a phone call. The next phase of evolution was arrival of internet based phone companies like Vonage. These companies provided an electronic box which was to be connected to the internet connection. The box required elaborate configuration before it could be ready to use. A telephone instrument could be connected to this box, it would have a permanent telephone number and it would be utilized to make phones like a regular land line. The device would covert the sound to internet based data and transfer it on the internet. The issue with this setup was that it required elaborate configuration knowledge and the setup was done at a particular location.

In 2008, a new system started becoming popular – MagicJack. This was a USB based device and looked like another USB based flash drive and had a phone jack on its one side, where a regular land line phone device could be attached. This device could be connected to any Personal Computer or Laptop anywhere in the world, and it would give the same telephone number to the user. This was like taking your land line with you anywhere in the world with this device and the receiving party would not know where you are making the call from. The device required no configuration by the user, and was very easy to use. The quality of the sound was dependent on the internet speed at the location of the user. However, an issue with this device was that you had to keep your personal computer or laptop always on, to use this device. Many times, if the user switched off his laptop computer, he would not be able to receive any phone calls.

To solve this problem, in 2011, the company came up with an enhanced version of this device, called the magicjack plus. This device could do the function required thru the personal computer also thru its firmware chip and it just needed a power supply. So now, you could plug this device in a power point, connect it to internet and plug your phone cable to it, to have a permanent internet based phone at home. The device was still a mobile device and you could go anywhere in the world with this device.

(The magicjack picture above shows that is connected to the USB port of a PC or laptop from one side, whereas a phone jack is available on the other side. In the case of a magicjack plus – picture is below, there is an additional ethernet port, so that an internet connection can be directly used from ethernet cable from the internet provider in one's home. This removes the need of a PC or laptop connection and keeping it on all the time)

Using Basic Research For Online Social Networking:

While internet had started becoming popular in early 1990s, the Industry realized the concept of social networking only in 2000s. It was based on the research done on the theory of 'six degrees of separation'. The theory says that almost any two people in the world are connected to each other through a 6 people link. In other words, if you take all the friends and contacts of a person in New York, and then look at all the friends and contacts of those people and this chain continues for around six times, it will reach almost the entire planet, except isolated groups of areas not connected through telecommunications. Using this research, the concept of LinkedIn.com was started in the 2000s which became popular. Using Linkedin, people started doing online networking and sharing their contacts with other friends online.

The same concept was further extended by Facebook, where users would share their pictures and their thoughts with their friends and allow their friends to share with other people. Facebook has later started profiling users based on their messages and the choice of the advertisements they have clicked previously to target potential customers for online products being sold.

The Importance of Basic Research:

It is difficult to create products with first mover advantage without utilizing new research based components. When Steve Jobs created iPhone, he utilized the multi-touch screen technology to give the product a first mover advantage. However, later, many Android based mobile phones utilized the same technology in an year's time, but they could not command the pricing power of Apple's iPhone. Just like deep understanding of a new research in technology is utilized, deep understanding of consumer behavior can also be utilized to create disruptive innovations. Just like Steve Jobs utilized the multi-touch screen concept to come up with iPhone, Mohammad Yunus utilized the understanding of social group behavior in Bangladesh to come up with the concept of micro-lending. Though the frameworks utilized to come up with innovative products are still the same, these products were not possible without these deep insights.

The cycle of innovation progresses with new research work being utilized to create new products, services and processes. Let me explain the importance of fundamental research in the process of Innovation by a very simple hypothetical problem:

John, a tourist from UK to United States is staying in Jersey city in New Jersey, USA near a train station, Journal Square. He has to go to the John F Kennedy Airport in New York. He needs to carry two large suitcases and an airport carry-on bag with him. He is wondering what is an inexpensive way to reach the JFK Airport? How would he come up with the best possible way to reach the airport?

His first attempt is to ask for Taxi fare from his home to the Airport. He comes to know that it is very expensive. He uses internet to find that a PATH train from Journal Square station would take him to New York and From New Yok, he can take the "A" Train to the Airtrain station of JFK Airport. From the Airtrain, he can go to his terminal by paying fees. This is the most inexpensive way to go to the JFK airport. Unfortunately, it would not be possible for him to go with 3 suitcases alone on the train. What now?

This is the time where the discovery processes need basic research to come into play:

Now, instead of finding ways to go from his home to JFK Airport, he goes to the website of JFK Airport to find out what are modes of transportation to and from the Airport. He comes to know that there is an Airport to Airport Shuttle from JFK to Newark Airport and vice versa. Since Newark Airport is near Jersey city, John realizes that he can take a Taxi to Newark Airport and then take the Airport to Airport Shuttle. This is cheaper than taking a direct Taxi from hotel to JFK Airport. Without doing a systematic search to identify a new mode of transportation, it was not possible for John to find out about this innovative process.

4

CONSUMER PSYCHOLOGY AND NEW PRODUCTS

. . . .

What innovations would sell?

After reading about the different frameworks of innovation in this book, the reader would feel that he has the option of doing many different types of innovations on every product and is wondering what innovation he should do that would sell?

Innovations can be done to fulfill a pent-up demand of the consumers, to satisfy a market trend or to fulfill a longer term goal of profitability. What innovation would sell immediately depends on the needs of different customers and the general trend in the economy. Here are a few important factors the innovator needs to consider to understand the market dynamics for a new product:

Filling in an obvious and everyday need:

Many products fill up a pent-up demand of consumers and therefore become instant success. Products which help save time, increase efficiency and save costs are these types of products. Such products become successful with little marketing efforts.

These products fill in an obvious and urgent need of the consumers and are helpful in fulfilling the everyday need of the consumers.

Almost all the products in 'Dollar Stores' in America are of such nature which are required by consumers for their daily need. Many of these products are never advertised on an individual basis. One would hardly see an advertisement for a a door-Hanger for clothes or a head-phone for a mobile phone? These are everyday needs of consumers and consumers search for these and purchase even when there are no advertisements.

However, the demand for such products in a particular region can be influenced by the local culture and needs of a place. The innovator needs to understand the reasons why the demand for a Wine-bottle-opener would be much higher in Europe than in a middle-east country. Similarly, Rural China would still prefer to use chopsticks to eat their food rather than a fork; and rural India would still prefer to use a turban instead of a western hat.

The demand for products also changes with a change in culture over time at the same place and the innovator needs to keep track of the changes in society. The demand for western products has been increasing for the last few decades in the developing countries. Similarly, the acceptability of foreign goods and services in United States has also increased in the same period.

I once saw a very innovative product being sold in Mumbai, India – it was a small instrument to easily enable putting a threat in a needle. The product was popular in the 90s among households, particularly the middle-aged women who have poor short-distance vision who were stitching or fixing clothes at home. As the culture of India has been changing, more people prefer ready-made garments than home stitched clothes and fewer women stitch clothes at home, the demand for this instrument has also gone down.

GPS (Global Positioning System) for navigation has become very popular in US to help drivers, though not yet in Asia. United

States owing to its large size, relatively thin population density and high speed highways is an ideal market for this product. On the other hand, Asian countries typically are smaller in size, are densely populated and have slow traffic. In most of the Indian cities, a car driver can just stop the car almost anywhere and ask for the directions to his destination. He would not need to use a GPS system there.

Another example is a door-top hanger for clothes, which we explained earlier in the chapter to explain about framework for alternative means. This product is used to hang clothes behind doors and is just put on the door and does not require any drilling or putting nails on the wall. Millions of these are sold in America every day, with no need of any advertisements by the producers. The product is simple and is just fulfilling an every day need.

Filling an event-driven need:

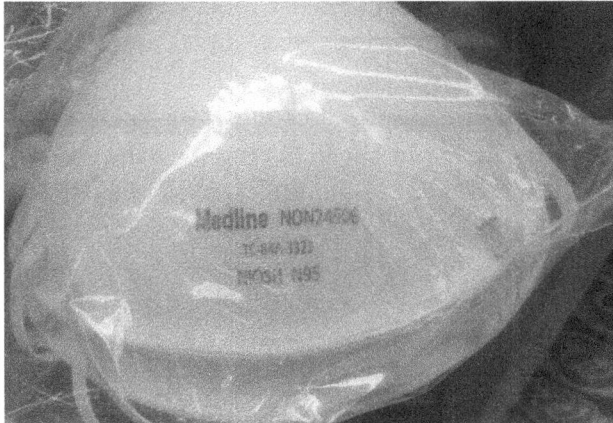

The N95 Masks became popular to protect from Swine Flu. These masks promise to be more effective than other masks and were imported by many Asian countries from HongKong in the summer of 2009 and consumers were willing to pay as much as ten times the actual price for a mask. Any company which could come up with a design with better protection would have also sold the product successfully.

Such products fulfill the urgent requirement of the consumer due to a particular event. Some of these products are seasonal and also dependent on weather conditions. A snow shovel is needed in snow and a leaf blowing machine is used in Fall season in America when people have to get rid of the leaves from their backyards.

The Innovating company for such event-driven needs has to be very agile to understand the need as well do the design, production and marketing of the product in a short time.

The Lifestyle Factor: Fulfilling a Hidden Need

Before the microwave oven was invented, perhaps no consumer ever went to a store and asked for a product like microwave that would heat food without using fire or direct heat.

Many such products can be created when there is no urgent need for the consumers to get that product. However, once such products are created, they generate demand. Creating products like these requires superior skills in understanding the non-obvious needs of consumers. Such products will also require marketing efforts to make the consumer aware of the usefulness of the product. These products gain mass popularity after the prices fall down to affordable levels for the masses. The average customer would not be able to conceive of such a product and would never demand for such product. The innovator would need to understand ergonomics and would need to identify what would provide the customer a feeling of ease for his requirements or work or pleasure.

Fluorescent lamp created its own demand due to the energy savings and the fact that the lamp pays for itself due to its longer life and cost savings. Bluetooth based Hands free headset for cellular phones is also a product of this category. Modern electronics like VCRs, Video Games etc are some of the examples of this type. Consumers had no obvious need for these before the products arrived in the market, but the demand was generated once the products were available at affordable prices.

Such type of lifestyle products became popular in the beginning primarily due to the prestige factor attached to their ownership and later become mass products as their prices fell down and they became affordable to masses. Some of these lifestyle products are VCRs, Color TVs in 1980s, Personal Computers in 1990s, the mobile phones, the iPods and the iPads in the 2000s.

While designing products like these, the innovator needs to do break-even analysis for covering the costs of product development, production and marketing.

Market Trends:

To understand how market trends can totally change the demand of consumers, let us look at an example from the car industry. In the US from mid 90s to beginning of 2000s, gasoline prices were low. Consumers demanded bigger cars which were comfortable and had powerful engines, though these were less fuel efficient.

Mini-vans and SUVs became popular in that decade. General Motor's Hummer H1 had a fuel economy of 12-16 miles per gallon and came in engine sizes larger than 6 liter.

(GM's Hummer in the picture above)

The hybrid car technology to make cars fuel efficient was developed by the Japanese in late 1990s and was available to be utilized in the cars. This hybrid engine technology had both an Electric engine as well as a Gasoline engine and a system where the idling power of the Gasoline engine would charge the electric engine. The fuel efficiency of this hybrid engine technology was almost two times the normal gasoline engines.

However, there were hardly any buyers for it in United States during the 1990s, as the consumers were not willing to spend extra money for the hybrid engine. Due to the low fuel prices, customers had little incentive to pay upfront a higher price for a hybrid engine to save on some fuel costs.

However, just a few years later, after mid 2000s, gas prices had increased by more than five times from the prices in late 1990s. (prices per gallon rose to more than $4 compared to around $0.70 in 1999). With recession from 2008 onwards, Consumers became cost conscious and started trading Mini-vans and SUVs with compact Sedans. Demand for Hybrid cars increased dramatically, and General Motors announced that it would stop producing Hummer H1...

From mid 2000s, anything which saved fuel consumption started becoming popular. Besides fuel efficient cars, the concept of fuel efficient homes started becoming popular. Many commercial buildings started getting the LEED GREEN BUILDING RATING CERTIFICATION developed by United States Green Building Council. LEED system redesigned everything in a building or home so that it minimizes the consumption of fuel and electricity. Many processes being utilized in Green buildings are very simple and based on common sense. For example, instead of putting an AC vent on the roof, it recommends putting it in the floor and putting the exhaust on the Roof. The Cold Air would stay near the floor to keep it cool and as it gets warmer, it would go up near the roof from where it can be moved out from the exhaust. Further, the buildings recommend large windows that utilized sunlight to save electricity.

So once the market favored "Green" technologies, many companies have created products to save on fuel costs.

Price Sensitivity:

It is important for the innovator to understand the price sensitivity of a customer. In 2002, a person known to me Michael (name changed) was doing his PhD in business management from a leading business school in New York. While doing this PhD, he studied the business model of StarBucks Coffee chain. He realized that Starbucks coffee is fulfilling the desire of people to taste gourmet coffee flavors in a luxurious environment. Michael further figured that Starbucks Coffee stores are almost exclusively in high income neighborhoods or in Commercial centers. He felt that Starbucks has been ignoring the lower income neighborhoods, as it probably did not see a potential of selling an expensive cup of coffee in these neighborhoods. Michael felt that there is a customer segment in these low income neighborhoods who would like to spend their money to purchase a high end gourmet coffee in a luxurious ambience. Michael was so excited by his analysis that he left his PhD in the middle to start his first coffee store. He identified a location quite close to the Journal Square train station in Jersey City and opened his first store, in 2004. This store was almost very similar in ambience to the Starbucks coffee stores. However, there were hardly any customers who entered his store during the first few weeks. Later, he even lowered the price of his gourmet coffee to half the price of a similar Starbucks Coffee in New York. Still, the store could not attract enough customers to break-even the costs. He had to close the business after nearly six months. He later confessed that he ignored the fact that customers in this neighborhood were very price sensitive. In-fact customers here even remembered which stores charge 75 cents for a cup of coffee and which stores charge 85 cents. Customers here were not willing to pay $1.50 per cup of coffee at that time, at least for a non brand coffee store like his.

Customer segmentation, customer surveys and price sensitivity are very important tools required to launch a new innovative product or concept.

The innovator needs to assess the amount of time required to recover the costs of building the new product and marketing it, as that is critical in making decisions whether to go ahead with building the new product.

Consider established Standards:

Before Apple made the smartphones popular with iPhone, one of the first PDA (Personal Digital Assistant) and smartphones came from a company Palm. The earlier versions of Palm expected users to learn certain strokes to be used in lieu of the letters. The Palm screen would decipher these strokes, which were similar to the letters as those letters. However, users found learning these new strokes inconvenient. Palm realized it and changed the design of its later touch screen based phones to accept input from a standard Qwerty keyboard. One Keyboard would appear on the touch screen as well as another one would flip out as an actual input device in the phone. Essentially, going against an established standard is very difficult as customers do not have inclination to learn newer processes and technologies. Many traditional investors and strategists cannot comprehend why certain companies like Amazon.com keep growing when it is not difficult to open competing book selling companies on Internet and there are so many competitors. These traditional investors have overlooked the fact that customers get used to a standard purchasing process on a particular website and unless there is a strong reason, they do not want to learn a new process on a new website.

Many times an established standard makes it difficult for a new product not conforming to this standard to compete in the market place. A person Alex (name changed) was working as a Sr Product Manager at a leading technology firm. He along with his few friends identified the problem of stealing of credit card numbers on the internet. They resigned from their companies and started a new company to design a solution to this problem. They utilized the Combination methodology framework by combining the constantly changing electronic token concept in lieu of the Card Security Code of the credit card. While making a payment on internet using a credit card, the Card Security Code is always asked, besides the credit card number and other details. This Card Security Code is generally a 3 digit number at the back of the credit card. All this information being asked on internet while making a payment is static data and can be stolen by hackers. Alex and his friends realized that if they use a constantly changing Card Security code, the hackers would not be able to use the remaining credit card information. Though the concept is great and uses proven technologies, Alex and his team have not been successful in convincing any bank to use their solution in the last few years. This is because of the resistance to change an industry standard. Changing an established standard is a difficult task and many good innovations would not be able to do so.

Providing Ease of Use/Ergonomics:

Many times consumers consider ease of use as an important factor in making a decision towards utilizing a new product or service. A hands free headset makes it easy for the user to talk for a long time without holding the phone. Similarly, for cellular phones, Sony designed ear phones which could be worn on ears, so that they do not fall even while running. A microwave oven makes it easy for you to heat your food.

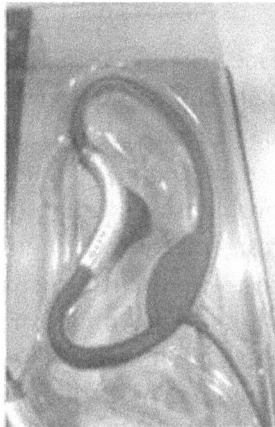

The picture above is that of the earphones from Sony which snug into the ears so that they do not fall and do not need to held with hands)

Cultural factors influence the need of consumers. SMS/text message based services have become very popular in Asia, but are largely not being used in USA. In fact, mobile commerce has also started becoming popular in Asia, but US consumers are still not showing inclination of using another form of making payments.

Two reasons could be attributed to the SMS based services not being popular in US compared to Asia, ergonomics and cultural reasons: Ergonomics, as people in Asia are generally smaller physically, have thinner fingers and therefore, and are comfortable using the small screen/keyboard of the mobile phones. With large touch screens provided by iPhone and Android Phones, this is slowly changing now only in the last two to three years.

It has been revealed by some surveys that people in the US are the most extrovert in the world and prefer to pick up a phone and speak to others rather than send text messages. On the other hand, Asians are generally considered introvert by nature, and therefore perhaps are at ease sending text messages to convey their message.

Many of the internet based businesses have got their processes of doing business patented. As an example, Amazon.com got the purchasing using one-click option patented in 1999.These businesses are aware that their processes are one of the easiest to use and provide a competitive strength to them.

Disruptive Innovation vs Incremental Innovation:

An e-book is a disruptive innovation that can be bought and sold digitally using internet and can be read on a personal computer or a reading device like an iPad or Kindle. The e-book replaces the need for a paper based book and gives a challenge to existing players in the paper based publishing industry. Many internet based businesses have been considered disruptive to existing players. Before the arrival of Amazon.com, people had to physically go to a Book Store and ask for a particular book. If the book was not available, the book store would either recommend another store or would order from his storage department. With Amazon.com, a customer can just order any book from the comfort of his home. Netflix has utilized the high speed internet connections available widely since 2000s, to sell movies and other entertainment material digitally. The effect has been closing down of thousands of video rental stores across United States. Emails have obviated the need of sending paper based messages using Postal Services and threatened their existence. In 2011, United States Postal services declared that 3700 post offices would be closed down, due to lack of sufficient business to justify their existence.

Some companies prefer to make changes to their existing products to make these more useful and acceptable to a wider set of consumers. Other companies prefer disruptive innovation which replaces existing set of products completely with an alternate way of getting the work accomplished. Disruptive innovation replaces existing set of market players with new dominant players. This innovation is what creates "creative destruction" in the economy, a term made popular by renowned economist Joseph Schumpeter.

Companies which are very small and have miniscule or negligible market share have much higher chances of growing if they come up with disruptive innovations. These companies would typically come up with new fundamentally new approaches to solving the needs of consumers.

However, large companies dominating the market with existing set of products prefer to ignore disruptive innovation as that would be displacing their own products' market dominance. These companies tend to think of adding functionality to their existing set of products and create complimentary products which serve additional needs of the consumers.

It is natural for large companies to continue to push its own technologies in-spite of arrival of a disruptive innovation in the market. Many times large companies will buy smaller upcoming companies with disruptive technologies just to kill the competition. Other times, it would try to grow its own revenues utilizing the new technologies.

When IBM's top management planned to create a personal computer, they had internal resistance against creating a disruptive technology and they had to utilize the services of Microsoft and Intel to make the prototype of a Personal Computer.

Later, in the late 1980s, when many companies started switching applications from a mainframe to a mini computer, IBM's market dominance suffered. However, with the arrival of Lou Gerstner as CEO of IBM, IBM started building on non-mainframe technologies. In the 1990s, IBM acquired many software companies like Lotus Notes which were primarily based on non-mainframe users. IBM was able to adapt itself to new disruptive technologies and grow business based on these new technologies. With giant corporations like Microsoft and Oracle having formed on the basis of either research or initiative of IBM, it is apparent that IBM had been avoiding disruptive innovation which was utilized by other companies to grow in new space. Many companies have realized this mistake and in order to ensure that they can track and stay on top of any disruptive technologies, have started their own Venture Capital Funds. Companies like Intel and Siemens have started their own venture capital funds to identify and invest in companies with new technologies which could either add to their product range or disrupt the market.

5

EXAMPLES

....

O ne of the first steps in developing the skills of innovation is the ability to identify patterns of innovation in the objects around us. We will understand the different frameworks of innovation using examples and essays. Using these examples, the reader would start identifying patterns of innovations in terms of different frameworks. The reader should try to understand the process that was used to design the product and comprehend the reasons for the need of these products.

ADDITION METHODOLOGY:

Addition Methodology is the easiest one to implement and can be observed in many products. In this methodology, the functionality of main product is enhanced by adding new technologies. In most cases, the target customer segment remains the same with this methodology.

Mobile Phones:

An example of this methodology is the constantly changing designs of mobile phones. While the earlier Mobile phones were simple devices to be used only for making phone calls, the manufacturers kept using addition methodology to add new features. It started with a Qwerty keyboard and an internet browser and have now added FM Radio and GPS Navigation system. A few other examples are explained here:

Coin Jar cum Piggy Bank with a Digital Counting Display:

As mentioned in the earlier chapters, an electronic counting device and a display has been added to the traditional children's Piggy bank cum Coin jar that shows the total money that has been inserted in the piggy bank. The value addition has been done on a traditional device to make it more useful and appealing to the customer.

Bottle net:

Many a times I have wondered how long can you continue to do innovation on a product to improve its functionality. The answer came to me via a small but beautiful product I recently came across.

It was while travelling from New York to New Delhi by an Air India flight. As I sat and looked in the front, I noticed a small 'bottle-net' near the floor, attached on the rear of the two seats in front of me.

This was a net to hold a water bottle. Without this net, I would have to keep my water bottle in the back-pocket behind my front seat. That pocket is usually very tight which crushes the plastic bottle and results in the passenger loosing a few inches of legspace.

This bottle net allowed me a few extra inches of leg space as it was on the side, between the 2 seats. The design was impressive as the net is strong, flexible and its visibility is good.

Though the inclusion of a bottle-net is not going to impact many people's decision on flying by an airline, small improvements like this add to a customer's comfort.

This product is so basic and simple that it could have been included in the first commercial aircraft, but the Industry took over half a century to realize its need, and nearly a decade after providing private LCD monitors for watching movies.

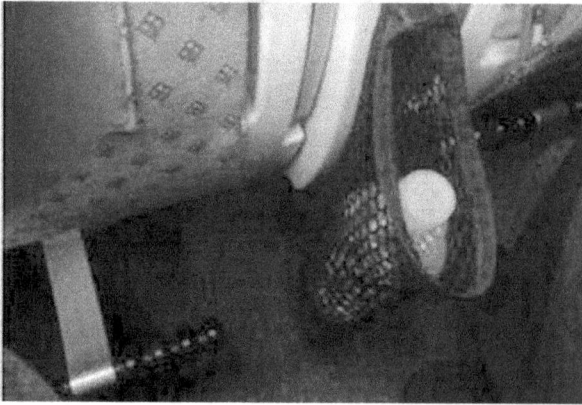

Frameworks: This product is added to the passenger seats to increases the convenience for passengers, it is an example of ADDITION METHODOLOGY and requires the skills to understand hidden non-obvious needs of the customer.

Cinemas with Beds:

The first time I saw a cinema theater with beds, pillows, comforters and side tables was in a smaller city in India, many years back. Here, waiters could bring you food and soft drinks on your side table. The beds could be adjusted to suit your comfort while watching the film. The ticket for this homelike-comfort was five times the regular price. Also, very recently saw an advertisement by a cinema theater in US. It has dinner tables and they can serve you food and drinks while you watch the movie. Perhaps, you can charge higher prices by increasing the level of comfort in any service.

Frameworks Used: Addition

Camera For Rear-View In A Car (http://backup4safety.com/):

If you are a cautious driver, you may find this product useful for your car – this is a rear license plate mounted camera with mount vision to protect little children while you are reversing the car. This camera gets activated when the car is put in reverse gear. This product is used to make older vehicles safe, as many newer vehicles come installed with this rear view camera.

Frameworks Used: Addition

SUBTRACTION METHODOLOGY:

BAJAJ's 200 CC Car:

India's Tata group had shocked the world markets in 2009 by announcing a very small car for only $2000. This car had a 2 cylinder 620 cc engine and it could carry up to 4 passengers. The Tata group had pitched this car for people using 2 wheelers (motorcycles and scooters).

The Bajaj group, the largest 2 wheeler company in India, decided to launch its own small car to compete with Tata's Nano. In 2012, Bajaj group announced the launch of RE60, a 200 cc car which would give 83 miles per gallon. The car weighs only 880 pounds and can carry up to 4 people. The car is a no frills car available at less than $3000 and would be targeted at customers of 2 and 3 wheeler vehicles. In India, a "three-wheeler" (a small vehicle with

3 wheels) is used like a taxi in most cities of India and Bajaj expects that many of these three- wheeler vehicles could be replaced by the RE60.

NYPD's T3 Electric Scooter :

The New York Police department has started using T3, a small electric scooter in the subway. This minimal scooter device serves the basic purpose of mobility. It does not even have a seat and a cop has to stand on it. Due to the minimal size, it can be used in narrow spaces in the subway.

ALTERNATE MEANS METHODOLOGY:

E-CIGARETTES:

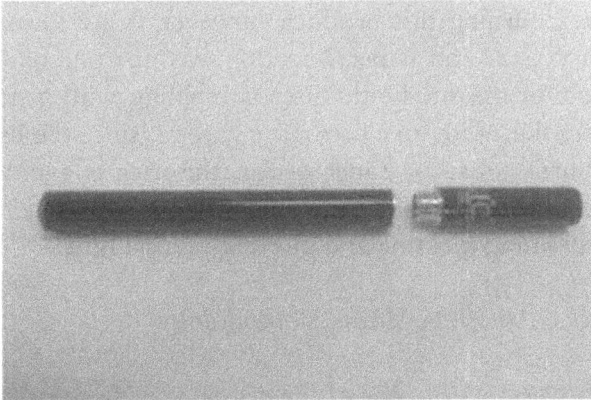

http://en.wikipedia.org/wiki/Electronic_cigarette

The concept of an electronic cigarette has started becoming popular in the last 5 years in United States. The product produces a mist of nicotine which the user inhales, in lieu of a paper based cigarette. It has been advertised that this is an alternative means of inhaling nicotine. This product saves the user from smoking a paper based cigarette, where the user is inhaling a burnt paper and burnt tobacco smoke and has much more harmful effects.

The product has 3 main parts:

- A cartridge holding a liquid to be vaporized

- An atomizer that servers as the heating element responsible for vaporizing the liquid

- A power supply, usually a battery.

The system works where the battery powered atomizer vaporizes the liquid into a mist containing nicotine, to be inhaled by the used. The liquid is usually glycol or glycerin with nicotine in it.

This product is an example of the alternate means methodology. Before this, the traditional route of getting nicotine has been wrapping the tobacco leaves in a paper roll, and inhaling the smoke after burning this product, however, it gives toxic fumes from tobacco, tar and paper. Nicotine was just one of the many components of the smoke the user is inhaling with a traditional cigarette smoke. With an electronic cigarette, since the user is not inhaling burnt tobacco, paper or tar, the user is avoiding their harmful effects. However, he would still be suffering from any effects of inhaling nicotine and glycol/glycerine mist.

Frameworks: Alternate Means Methodology

Solar Power for Rural Indian Homes:

Duron Energy, is a Bangalore based company in India, it is backed by Idealab, USA. The company is focusing on providing Solar power based solutions to rural homes in southern parts of India. The company identified that warm weather in that geography generates demands for use of a fan and these households also need an electric light bulb in the evenings

It is also a fact that India offers one of the cheapest wireless service plans in the world, making wireless communication affordable. While landlines are not yet available, most homes have cellular phones and these require regular recharge of batteries.

To fulfill the power needs of these areas, the company introduced its product- DURON BREEZE, a solar power backed battery system. The fully powered battery, when used alone for a fan, allows it to run for 7 hours.

2 LED based efficient light systems are being used instead of traditional electric bulb (which consumes more electricity generating heat than generating light). It also has an equipment to charge cellular phone. All of these 3 equipments can be used simultaneously for 4 hours with Duron Breeze.

Frameworks: All Alternate energy based products are examples of Alternate Means Methodology

TIRE SEALANT - Instant Tire Repair:

SLIME: A need was identified to find a way to repair a small leakage in the car's tire instantly. Slime, a solution to this problem is a tire sealant that comes in a liquid form and is inserted in the Tire. It remains in the liquid form for nearly 2 years. The product instantly repairs a small puncture.

The company's web site explains the process as :

"As the SLiME treated tube rotates, centrifugal force pushes the sealant to the tread area creating a layer of protection, repairing punctures as they occur or treating existing punctures. SLiME is not intended for use in tubes losing pressure from sidewall punctures, bead leaks, damaged rims or faulty valves. SLiME for tube type tires is NOT recommended for use in tubeless tires."

Fix a Flat: A similar product 'Fix a flat' has been created by another company, but this one is used to fix it after the puncture has happened. A pressurized bottle with a chemical is used to fill inside the tire. This chemical settles around the puncture area to clog the hole as a temporary fix.

Frameworks: The makers of these products identified a chemical product which could be utilized from inside the Tire to fix any small puncture instantly. This is an example of Alternate Means Methodology, and it required skills of understanding a non-obvious need and identifying a chemical product to satisfy the need.

MAKE IT MORE RUGGED:

I noticed RYOBI TEK4 in a Home Depot store. RYOBI TEK4 is an enhanced digital camera product. It is made as a very rugged product making it ideal for construction workers and architects working on tall building projects. It has many advanced features including:

- Strong casing and lens. It does not break even if the camera falls on a hard surface.

- Longer life battery: 800 photos can be taken per charge of battery

- Large ergonomic designs and buttons for easy handling for larger hands

- Voice memo recorder – useful for construction worker

Frameworks: This is an example of Alternate-means methodology where first a non-obvious need of having a stronger product for construction work was identified and then alternate materials were utilized to create this rugged camera.

Wet Umbrella Wrapper:

On one of the rainy days in New York, I saw a beautiful product at the entrance of a company – the product is a "Wet Umbrella Wrapper": This product is developed by understanding a need of the company to protect the office from the rainwater on the Umbrellas on rainy days. The product has sheets of plastic wrapper one over the other in this metal device. One can just insert the umbrella from the top to get it wrapped from this plastic wrapper and pull it out. The design makes it very easy to use and any water dripping from the umbrella stays within this plastic wrapper and does not make the floors of the office wet.

The innovator realized that many office floors get wet during rainy season and there is a need for an inexpensive way to save the floors from wet umbrellas. In smaller offices or stores, they keep a bucket at the entrance where people can keep the folded umbrella, so that all water stays within the bucket. However, this does not work in large multi-storied buildings where people carry their umbrellas to their floors. The need which this device fulfills are non-obvious needs of the consumer. Such needs are never stated by anybody and require good requirements-gathering and judgment skills of the innovator.

Frameworks: This product is created by understanding a non-apparent need and the product also works as a replacement for the traditional bucket at the entrance, it is an example of ALTERNATE MEANS METHODOLOGY.

Wankel Engine:

This is an example of an innovation methodology being used in research work. Traditional internal combustion engine was based on a design where a piston based reciprocating movement fed energy into a rotating motion. An alternate and more energy efficient design is in Wankel engine. This engine does not have piston strokes but here rotary motion of the engine is done by four phases of the intake, compression, ignition and exhaust at separate locations of this circular engine. This engine is primarily used in Mazda Cars.

Frameworks: Alternate Means Methodology

Sapphire Crystal Glasses for Watches:

The appearance of watches diminishes if there are scratches on the glass of the watch. To make it scratch-resistant watch companies started using Sapphire Crystal. Sapphire Crystal appears like glass but is so strong that it does not get scratched, even if you try to rub a steel knife on it. Initially, it was very expensive but the price of Sapphire Crystal has come down many folds in the last decade.

Frameworks Used: Alternate means methodology

Retractable Queue Equipment:

A retractable queue equipment is an equipment used mostly on the airports and in supermarkets to organize queues in the desired shape with minimum efforts. It is an equipment for guidance of public and crowd control. The equipment makes the size of the queue flexible and it is easy to setup and organize queues. Before this equipment, there used to be ropes and steel chain based queue equipment. The innovator realized that crowds at such places are highly disciplined, the crowd simply needs a guidance for direction and you do not need to utilize steel chains and ropes.

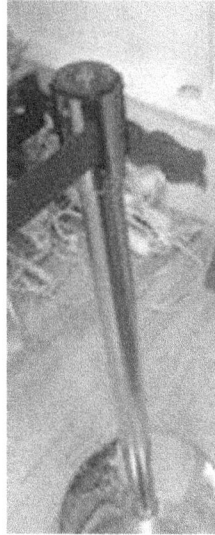

This patented product is one of those products which are simple and create a demand for themselves.

Frameworks: This product is created as a replacement of traditional ropes and steel chains based queues, so it is an example of ALTERNATE MEANS METHODOLOGY.

NJTRANSIT's 2 Sided Chair:

When we are travelling in a train, we are either facing the front or facing the rear. If a chair makes you face the front , the same chair will make you face the rear on the return journey. This is because the engine is simple moved from one end of the train to the other end on the return journey. Many passengers dislike facing the rear side of the train and would rather be facing the front. It was a pleasant surprise to find an NJ TRANSIT car where the chair could bes witched from front to reverse facing by moving the back rest, which also adjusted the seats accordingly. The designer of this adjustable chair must have been very good in understanding the non-obvious needs of the customers.

(the chair is adjusted to face the front of the train)

(the chair is now adjusted to face the rear of the train)

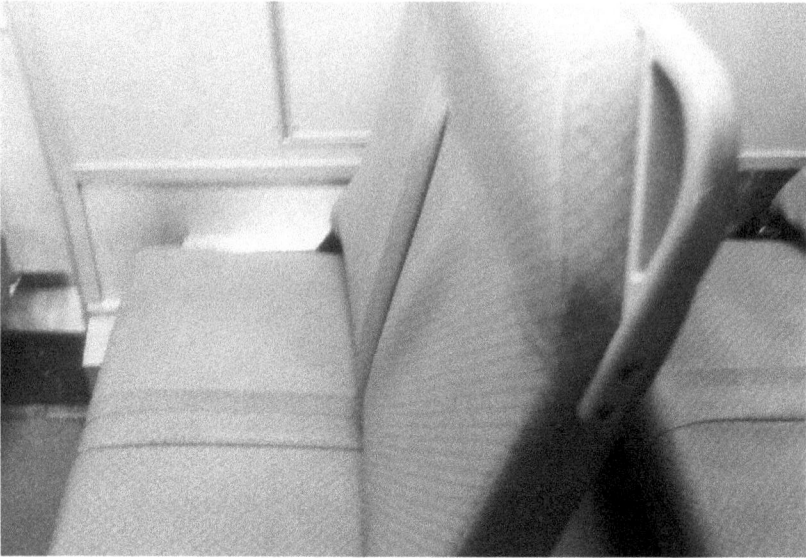

(The above Pictures were taken in a train)

COMBINATION METHODOLOGY:

When two separate products are combined to create a new product or enhance the product to target a new customer segment, the methodology is called a combination methodology.

Need to smell bombs? Use Bees:

While new technologies were being identified to create a device for sensing a bomb, it was realized that bees have a very accurate sense of smell. Now the question was how to train a bee to tell us if it smelled a bomb. The technique that is utilized to train a dog based on rewarding it with a biscuit when it sniffed a particular smell was also utilized on bees. The bees were captured and then trained to signal the smell of detonation material.

Then a small container was created containing bees and a miniature camera. The camera would detect the signal of the bees and create an electronic alarm when they sensed the bees.

From:http://gizmodo.com/299525/bomb-detector-powered-by-bee-tongue

"The company literally trains bees as a police force might train dogs. Using Pavlovian principles, the bees are given a food reward when they sniff, let's say, cocaine. Over time, the bees are conditioned to stick out their tongues in hunger over the smell of this substance. Then, in a highly scientific operation, the bees are taped to your measurement device. A camera closely tracks the bee tongues while the you pray that the SWAT team really is on their way (lest you need to release your "measurement device" for self-defense)."

Frameworks: Combination methodology of innovation.

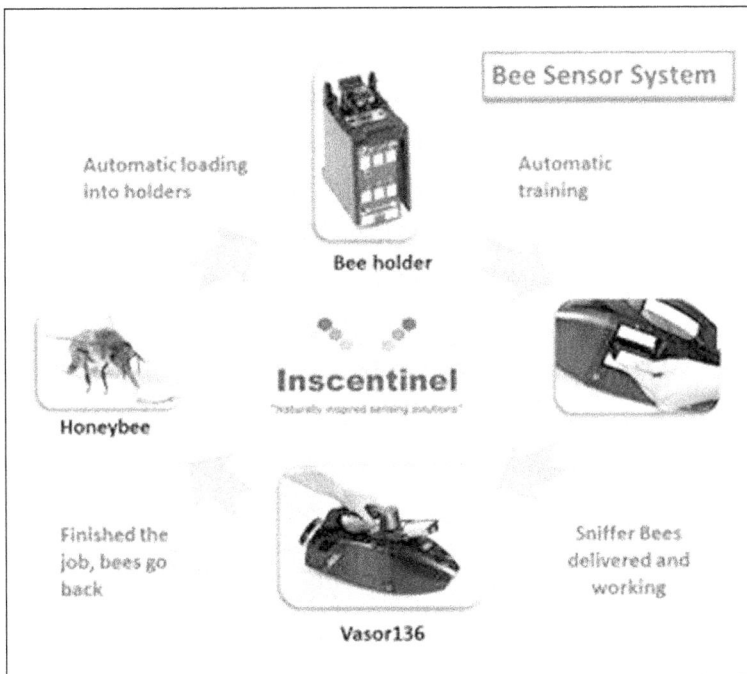

The above picture is with the courtesy of rothamsted research, UK.

Electronic Soap Dispenser:

A few years back, I was watching the biopic of Howard Hughes 'Aviator' about the famous aircraft aviator and engineer. In one scene, Leonardo Dicaprio, playing the role of Howard Hughes is waiting near a bathroom door waiting for someone else to open the door. He was paranoid of catching bacteria by touching anything in the bathroom. More than half a century later, solutions for such issues are available.

With increasing education about the many types of bacteria and virus, many people have become hyper-sensitive about germs and some people are almost paranoid about catching germs in a public toilet. To assuage such feelings, an electronic Soap Dispenser has been designed. It dispenses soap based on the principles of photo-sensitivity, so that people do not have to touch the soap dispenser.

Frameworks: The product uses combination methodology by combining a Photo-sensitive electronic device and a soap dispenser. It required understanding the need of certain people who are overly cautious from any bacteria getting transmitted, while touching the soap dispenser. This is still not being used by everyone and is being used in large hotels and offices.

MITEK: Electronic Cheque Deposit:

Mitek provides a mobile phone based software solution to deposit bank cheques using mobile phone. It utilizes the modern features of smartphones like Apple's iPhone and Android based phones to install the software applications and the high quality cameras. It also combines the power of 2 factor authentication and encryption for additional safety of image being captured and being transferred to the bank.

A user takes the picture of the front and back of the cheque using his phone's camera and verifies the quality of the picture. It also uses the OCR (Optical Character Recognition) software for MICR validation. The image is transferred to the banks, thereby instantly depositing the cheque in the account of the user.

Frameworks Used: Combination

TRANSPOSITION METHODOLOGY:

As explained earlier, in late 19th century, when the concepts behind a bird's flying were being studied to be applied to the design of an airplane, they were using transposition methodology. Transposition methodology is the most powerful innovation methodology utilized to create disruptive innovation. This methodology requires taking the traits of a product and applying them to another product to design a new product.

A few examples:

SWIMMING ON A TREADMILL:

The concept of a treadmill has been applied to an indoor small swimming pool to make a swimming machine. The swimming machine is a resistance swimming equipment enabling the swimmer to swim in one place. This countercurrent swimming machine works by accelerating the water past the swimmer. The swimmer swims in a small pool against a jet of water with adjustable flow where the flow is managed by mechanical pumps or propeller driven machines. This enables the swimmer to constantly swim while still being at one place.

Frameworks: Transposition Methodology

Fresh Juice Vending Machines:

The weather in NY Metro area becomes hot in summers - above 90 F on many days. While traveling around the metro area by public transportation - there is limited choice for soft drinks - you can get packaged soft drinks, water and juices from vending machines, but if you want fresh juice, it is generally not available.

A few specialty stores do offer fresh juice, but it is very expensive due to the labor costs. All the technology to make fresh juice making vending machines is available, and I do see some online ads about it in other countries - but is yet to be commercialized in US.

Perhaps a vending machine can be created which will pick up chopped pieces of fruit, just like some of the claw crane based soft toy vending machines. It would then insert the picked fruit pieces in a juicer, and the customer would get a fresh glass of juice.

Frameworks Used: Addition and Transposition

Future Electronic reading devices:

An important difference between reading a paper book and reading a book on your laptop screen is that the laptop's screen emits light, which makes your eyes get tired in a short time.

Though a paper book needs an external light source to read it, it is normal for eyes to read a paper book for many hours without feeling tired. However, in the case of computer screens, since light is coming out of the laptop screen, our eyes get tired much faster by reading from a laptop screen.

Amazon.com realized this difference and created Kindle, an e-book reading device. This device combines the children's doodle technology with an electronic paper display process. It also utilizes Wi-Fi and mobile data networks to download files, allows bookmarks to be made in the e-book and has a software to read books, thus allowing listening to e-books.

In the future, regular laptop screens would probably get modified to include kindle-like features. Or kindle would be modified to allow internet-browsing using the e-Ink. A software protocol to convert from HTML documents to an e-ink based screen would probably be required for this enhancement.

A second way of doing enhancement could be done by utilizing an enhanced low intensity LED screen in such devices where light does not emit out of the screens, which would allow regular internet browser capable notepads to be used for reading e-books, giving the same experience as a Kindle.

Frameworks Used: Combination and Transposition

QR (Quick Response) Codes:

QR code is a two dimensional matrix barcode that was first designed for automotive industry in Japan. With the popularity of smart phones with camera, these QR codes are now being used during advertisements so that people can save the web addresses of companies by just clicking the picture of the barcodes on the hoardings.

(The picture above is the picture of a QR Code used in an advertisement)

Frameworks Used: Transposition

PROCESS INNOVATION METHODOLOGY:

Process innovation is about making changes to existing processes to enable efficiency.

Separate Lanes For Buses:

Many cities, including New York, have created separate bus lanes to be used by public buses during office hours.

The concept is simple and is used to encourage people to use public buses in lieu of private vehicles, as these buses are able to travel faster during peak office hours.

3 D Printing – Process innovation in manufacturing:

One of the traditional manufacturing processes involves taking a block of material and shaping it to the desired shape by reducing unneeded material. This may be called a reduction based methodology of giving shape to the material. This process was labor intensive. However, with the cost of robotic equipment going down in the last decade, an additive process has started becoming popular for manufacturing. Here molten plastics and fiber material are slowly added to give the desired shape using robotic equipment. This process is called a 3 D printing and is being seen as the future of manufacturing in the developed countries.

Saving electricity by feeder separation and scheduling:

Emerging countries having been struggling with meeting the demands of electricity due to limited generation capacity and fuel supplies. In the state of Gujarat, India, government identified that almost 35% of electricity to rural areas was being lost during distribution. The government identified that though electricity was supplied to both village homes as well as farms, only rural homes needed the electricity supply on a 24 hour basis. The farms need electricity only during certain times for irrigation. In order to reduce the distribution losses, Government of Gujarat separated the feeders for homes and farms. While homes are being supplied power all 24 hours during the day, power to farms is supplied only for some pre-scheduled periods for irrigation purposes. This feeder separation and scheduling has reduced the distribution losses from 35% to below 15%.

Finance work aggregation portal:

I met Khanan Grauer, promoter of financial portal http://fingad. com/ during a guest speaking event in New York. Despite so many financial portals in the market, he way trying something unique - though still at an early stage.

His pitch:

"Benjamin Graham, the father of value investing took five years to identify the talent and offer a job to Warren Buffet - the next greatest value investor. Most investment professionals are hired on wall street in less than 5 hours.

Fingad will aggregate the work of people doing investment to find top talent in the marketplace"

Besides aggregation and collaboration among his users for financial strategies, he was working on providing tools on his portal which the financial Industry insiders use for analysis. With so many scandals and bubbles bursting on wall street, there should be some new demand to utilize his website.

Frameworks Used: Tries to fill a non-obvious need, uses Transposition methodology

INNOVATIONS FOR SURVIVAL IN SMALL VILLAGES:

People in many rural areas, especially in developing countries have poor income. There, people are forced to experiment and come up with new innovative ways for their everyday needs. Having travelled to some of these villages in India, I admired the simple processes they have come up with and will share some of these:

Ice storage with no refrigerator:

In villages in India, a refrigerator is too expensive for most people. As it gets very hot during summers, some people purchase ice from market for their homes. However, the ice can melt fast in hot weather and they have to find a way to keep it for a long duration. I noticed that a family purchased a large brick of Ice, instead of ice cubes and then stored it in a room filled with hay for their cattle. This hay works as a multiple-layer protection for the ice. I came to know that in-spite of very high temperatures outside, the hay protects the Ice from melting for nearly two days.

How to create a wall inside a well:

When a well is dug, a circular wall of brick has to be laid on its inside boundary. This brick layer is important as it protects the mud from falling in the well. However, there is an issue here. Once you have dug the well to reach the water level, since it is water at the bottom, How do you do start the work of laying the bricks when there is no floor? There is no solid surface from where you can start the brick laying work. The Village masons use an interesting process to solve this problem. After digging a few feet of well (usually in a cylindrical shape), he lays the brick wall. Then as the well is dug further, he starts removing earth from the bottom of this brick wall in a special way, so that this cylindrical layer of brick starts sliding down. More bricks are laid from the top on this cylindrical structure, and the process continues till the bricks reach the water level. So, while it was not possible to start the brick laying from the bottom, this process of starting the brick laying from the top and sliding the cylindrical wall was a process innovation of alternate route.

How to store water for many years in an arid place:

Many villages in the state of Gujarat, India are in semi-arid zones, where rain falls every couple of years. One such village in kutch, Gujarat uses underground tanks. Homes in this village have drainage from roofs connected to the underground tanks. People let the rain wash the roof first for some period, and later open the drainage to the underground tank. They also use a local chemical to preserve water. This chemical saves the water from getting any bacterial growth for up to 3 years.

Barter System in this day and age:

I was travelling to one of the villages in the state of Haryana, near New Delhi. An Apple vendor came to the village. Perhaps, this vendor had realized that women and children are his main customers during the day time and they do not have much money to spend, but most families do farming so would have food grains stored in their home. This vendor was not charging money but was taking wheat for the Apples he was selling. Though barter system is there for thousands of years, identifying its demand and utilizing it in this day and age for trading is commendable.

Lighting Fire without a Matchbox:

It would be hard for many people to believe that the cost of a matchbox is considered expensive by many people in villages of emerging countries. These villagers ensure that they get fire stored inside the ashes of the burnt wood. By blowing air into the burnt wood, they get the fire in a piece of paper which they utilize to start their cooking process. Once in a while when this does not work, they ask their neighbors for the fire. Watching these villagers reminds one of the ancient times.

Cow Dung for Producing BioGas:

Cow's Dung is used in many ways in India. It was used as a manure (agriculture fertilizer) and as a fuel. Villages in India traditionally used to make Cakes and Dry them from Cow Dung and use it as a fuel for burning and cooking. However, as it was realized that they release methane gas, small bio-gas plants have been installed in many houses with cattle. This small plant requires around 5 feet by 5 feet of area in the backyard and has a gas pipe line connected to the kitchens. The Cow dung is put in this plant from one side, where the methane gas gets generated and collected in a chamber. Later, the decomposed cow dung is utilizes as a manure. Though Cow dung was being used as a fuel for a long time, utilizing it to get bio-gas was achievable with the support of the scientific community and is an example of alternate means methodology.

6

INDUSTRY BASED CASE STUDIES

. . . .

In this chapter we will discuss how an individual Industry and its products have evolved over the past and will also try to understand the changes in those products in reference to the innovation frameworks we have studied in the previous chapters. This would help the reader enhance his thought process about innovation in a particular product with reference to the innovation frameworks and consumer psychology.

INNOVATIONS IN FINANCE

Before the emergence of modern banking system and single currency system in United States, people had to carry with them Gold, Silver or other precious material while travelling long distances. People travelling short distances in boats or horse carriages also used to carry liquor for barter purposes, as Alcohol is non-perishable and was widely accepted in most places. United States has witnessed tremendous innovations in the finance Industry since then.

Financial innovations have helped people and corporations get access to the required capital for personal and business needs and thus helped the economy. Conversely, investors have got many options of getting returns on their capital based on their risk appetite and long term plans. Innovations in finance are basically about two parties: one needs access to capital and the other is providing capital with an expectation for a return on this capital. A new Innovation in finance invariably means creation of a new legal agreement between these two parties. These new agreements need to be enforceable by the legal system in that region. Therefore, many times innovations in finance require modifications in the local laws where innovations will be used. At times, some of these Innovations have also encouraged irresponsible behavior of consumers and corporations for capital and created speculative bubbles in the economy, the last famous one being the housing market in United States. Other times, the implications of these innovations are not understood by the governments and can result in catastrophic impacts on the economy, for example the Credit Default Swap and other Derivative instruments which were misused before the last recession.

Financial entities and instruments:

One of the earliest successful innovations in finance was the concept of a corporation. Instead of an investor either giving a loan to a business or becoming a partner in loss and profits of the business, the investor purchased shares of the business. With this instrument, the investor got share in the profits of the corporation, but was not personally liable for any losses more than the money invested in purchasing shares. Besides sharing profits in the form of dividends, shareholders also had voting rights in electing the managers and making important policy decisions. This more than 500 years old concept was modified in the 20th century by the introduction of class A and class B shares. The subtraction framework of innovation has been applied to reduce some of the functionality of common shares to create class B shares (the original common shares now being called class A shares). Class A shares were the common shares having right to vote as well as right to share in the dividends. However, Class B shares were the common shares with only right to dividends and no right to vote. This concept was utilized by founders of organizations who wanted to ensure that they do not loose decision making authority in their board meetings from investors who purchased common shares later. One of the most famous persons utilizing the concept of Class B shares is Mr Warren Buffet. His company Berkshire Hathaway acts as a holding and investment company. He has raised money to invest in new companies from common shareholders but would not like to lose control of the decision making in the Berkshire Hathaway. Therefore, very few shareholders have the class A shares in Berkshire Hathaway and most investors have only class B shares which are common shares but with no voting power. The class B shares have functionality which is a subset of the class A shares and is an example of subtraction based innovation methodology.

There are many periods, such as an early stage of launching a new product, in the lifecycle of a company which are considered high risk by investors. During these periods, some investors want to minimize the risk to their investment and prefer to get a fixed return. For these investors one option could be a Preferred share: a preferred share pays a fixed dividend to the investor. Common share holders are only paid from the remaining profits, if at all. However, the preferred shares do not have voting rights. Also, if after the fixed dividends of preferred share holders are paid, the remaining distributable profits are high, dividends paid to common shareholders could be higher than the dividends paid to preferred share holders.

Many investors wanted to invest in preferred shares to minimize their risk during certain periods and get at least a minimum return during that period, but then wanted to get the same rights as common shareholders after a few years. For these investors, the concept of convertible preferred shares was created. These preferred shares giving a fixed dividend but no voting rights are convertible to common shares after a few years. The shares are convertible on a pre-defined formula mostly based on the profitability of the company. Now, what if the company is still not making the expected profits after those few years? The investor still may not like to convert his preferred shares to common shares in this case. For these investors, the concept of optional convertible preferred shares was created. These preferred shares may or may not be converted to common shares, the option is given to the investor, after a particular period. If the company becomes highly profitable, it makes sense for the investor to convert his preferred shares to common shares as he will get voting rights and can get higher dividend than the preferred shares. On the other hand, if the company is still not enough profitable, it is better for the investor to keep getting a fixed dividend every year. These preferred and convertible preferred shares are an example of a need based innovation.

Some investors invest for a lifetime of returns via fixed dividends, but some investors want to get their invested capital back after a number of years. For the latter, the concept of redeemable preferred shares has been created. The invested capital is returned back to the investors of these preferred shares after a particular number of years.

Some investors lend money to companies by purchasing a financial instrument, a Bond. The interest may be fixed or floating, where the interest rates change as per the market conditions (like LIBOR rates). Unlike preferred shares which may or may not be redeemable, bonds have a fixed maturity date. The principal amount is returned back to the investor on that date. The interest on bonds could be paid on a fixed intervals, but could also be paid cumulatively at the time of maturity.

These innovations in finance have been done based on the obvious need of the customer or investor.

Credit Card:

The concept of a credit card first came into the existence in the 1920s, when cars became popular in America and people started travelling long distances. Finance industry in United States realized that customers might need money hundreds of miles away from their homes and many merchants may not accept the bank cheques. The concept of a credit card started in 1920s, but did not become popular till 1950s. A credit card offers short term credit to the customer and is an unsecured loan.

The concept of a Credit Card is based on combination methodology of innovation. It is created by joining the concepts of authentication based on an algorithm utilizing the credit card number and using a telephone line for communication to allow short term lending by a financial entity. The financial entity issuing the credit card is making two strong assumptions. First, that the merchant charging the credit card has verified the Identification of the customer and second that the customer is willing and capable of paying back the money to the financial entity. While the first risk is covered by looking at the past behavior of the merchant and by keeping a time lag between the time the credit card is charged and the time the money is paid to the merchant. To cover the second risks, the credit card is offered based on the concept of "creditworthiness" of an individual. Before the credit cards came in mass usage, they were offered to only people with "high status". Later, the credit card companies started monitoring the financial behavior of the customer and made decisions according to it. In 1990s, credit card companies tried to make it a mass market financial instrument, and lowered the credit requirements of many customers. Further, there was not a quick coordination between various credit card companies, and a person could carry and overspend from tens of credit cards with him simultaneously. The result of this unscrupulous behavior is now well known to the markets !

Micro Credit:

While unsecured credit started in United States, and the credit card was given to people based on their reputation and financial standing, the concept of micro-credit was invented in a developing country, Bangladesh. Professor Mohammad Yunus, the founder of Grameen Bank in Bangladesh realized that many people who were not considered credit-worthy as they were poor might be able and willing to pay back the credit granted to them, if given a chance. He started identifying poor people who had the willingness and ability to return the capital, and started giving them small loans. In order to put some social pressure on the individuals, he gave loans to a group of people knowing each other. That way, there was a collective responsibility of the people to return the capital. This Industry now known as microcredit has witnesses maximum growth in the 21st century.

Professor Mohammad Yunus has been awarded a Nobel Prize for his contribution and many companies have followed his model across the world. A financial innovation like this was possible because Professor Yunus deeply understood both the need of the consumer as well as the social behavior of people in his country. The concept may not work in all regions of the world, particularly in individualistic societies, as the acceptable social behavior and norm might be different there.

Structure of Funds:

Financial companies managing funds are somewhat different from other businesses. Venture Capital, Private Equity and Hedge Funds are financial companies managing funds of the investors. The investors in these funds are usually Pension organizations, University Endowment funds, large banking institutions and sometimes government organizations. The money invested by these entities in these financial funds is based on the reputation and trust of the top management persons of these financial funds. A wrong investment by these fund managers could lead to large losses to the investors in these funds. The structure of a traditional corporation allows the top managers to simply resign and leave the organization, which would have given too much freedom to fund managers to leave the organization with no liability after making wrong investment decisions. This led to the rise of another structure of business called Limited Liability Partnership structure. In this structure, the Fund managers raising the funds from investors are called General Partners who are bound to stay in the business till the fund's pre-defined operational period, usually around 7 to 10 years. The fund managers raise money from private investors and institutions (non stock market) for investing money in particular geographic areas and in certain market segments. These managers are also liable for any losses caused due to gross negligence and making investments. On the other hand, the investors in these funds are called Limited Partners as they are not liable for anything more than the investment they have made in these funds. The limited partners are not supposed to be involved in the day to day operations of the fund, but are informed by General partners about the operations on a regular basis.

Valuations:

The now infamous Enron Corporation misused an accounting rule that allows adding the profits of a wholly owned company to the parent company's profits. Enron sold and bought back a real estate asset to its wholly owned company giving the wholly owned company a large profit. Since it was a capital expenditure on Enron's books, it did not affect the earnings of Enron. On the other hand, the wholly owned company's profit was added to Enron's own profits, as allowed under the accounting rules.

Due to such peculiar rules in accounting, finance industry has been struggling to find a best method of valuing a company.

A number of innovations in valuations area in finance (both in positive and negative ways) have been possible due to the various and peculiar rules of accounting. Accounting rules recognize revenue and profit if the product has been sold to the customer, irrespective of the whether the payment has been received by the customer. Many times a product is sold to customer and the customer is not willing to pay the money back. In this case, the company should consider this default as deduct this amount from its Revenue calculations, thus reducing the profits. But many times, the company does not do this and keeps such sales on books (as Accounts Receivables), thus artificially boosting the Profits on Book.

The second accounting rule is the difference in the way a Cash spent is considered an Expense versus a Capital Expenditure. If a Cash is spent in routine administrative work and in the production costs of the Product or Service, it is considered an Expense and is subtracted from the Revenues to arrive at Gross Profit. However, if the same Cash is spent in purchasing Equipment, Land or a long term Asset, it is considered a capital expense and it is not deducted from the Revenue for calculations of the Profit. For many of these purchases, there is a difference of opinion among various accountants about what can be considered a Capital Expenditure and what is considered a routine Expense. This difference can change the Profits on Book of a company. Many companies and their accountants are inclined to consider a cash outflow as a Capital Expenditure to show higher profits on the books of the company.

Value investors like Mr. Warren Buffet have identified the issues in these peculiar accounting rules and they carefully read the annual statements of companies to segregate what is profit as per accounting rules and what may be considered profit as per the actual cash flows of the company.

On wall street however, routine valuation frameworks utilize the concepts of Earnings or Profit after Tax, EBITDA (earnings before interest taxes depreciation and amortization) or Gross Profit, Revenues, Cash Flow statements and sometimes in the case of internet companies the number of web page visits by potential customers. These figures are multiplied by a factor based on the Industry and market conditions to be utilized for valuation of the company.

One of the methods of valuation is done based on the concept of an earnings multiple, where the net profit of the company is multiplied to a factor to come up with the valuation of the equity. This factor could be based on the stock market based multiple of similar companies. Since this value is only the value of the equity, the debt of the company is added to this value to value the entire company as the purchaser would have to pay for both the equity as well as the debt of the company.

Another method of valuation is based on the Gross Income of the company, or EBITDA. This is the income of the company, before any interest, taxes, depreciation or amortization is deducted from this gross income. Again, a factor is multiplied to this EBITDA number to come up with a valuation of the company.

A third method of valuation is based on the future cash flows of the company. Using a set of assumptions about the revenues, expenditures and capital expenses, expected future cash flows of the company are calculated and then these numbers are discounted by a factor based to come up with Present values (PV) of these cash flows. The discounting factor is based on the expected returns on the investment. The sum of these Present values of these cash flows is considered for the valuation of the company. This methodology is very popular on the wall street. However, this methodology is criticized by many leading investors including Mr Warren Buffet as it is based on assumptions about the future cash flows of the company and it is very difficult to accurately predict the future of any company. The second issue with this methodology is that expected return from a company is based on many assumptions and these assumptions can be easily changed by the person doing the valuation. A slight variation in this expected return can change the Present Value calculations by a large margin.

Mortgage, Home Equity and Reverse Mortgage:

Before the concept of a mortgage became popular, a home buyer had to pay the full price of a house in cash to purchase it. Many home buyers had to save for decades before they could purchase their first home. Many times the home prices increased at a faster rate than the general inflation or wages and therefore making it almost impossible for many customers to purchase their homes. In the beginning, banks started giving loans by keeping a collateral which was another fully paid property of buyer. Banks could sell this existing property of the home buyer to recover their money if the buyer did not return the money and interest to the bank on time.

Finance Industry in the western world, particularly United States realized that as the value of homes usually keep increasing, loans can be provided to a home buyer to purchase the home, by keeping the home *to be purchased* as a collateral with the lender. In case of a buyer not paying back the loans to the bank, the banks can sell the property and recover their money from the sale price. This concept led to the growth of the mortgage industry. The concept got support from the legal systems in the western world where recovering money by selling the mortgaged property was easy as per the laws. However, the developing world took nearly fifty years before the banking and legal systems became mature to allow such type of transactions, an important reason being the socialist nature of laws in many developing countries.

With time, another concept – the concept of a home equity was created. Finance Industry realized that besides a fully paid house that has a lot of capital locked in it, even homes that have mortgage also have some unlocked capital. Since in a home loan or mortgage, a loan is given to the owner up to some percentage of the value of the house (usually upto 80% in United States), around 20% of the value of the home is still unlocked capital.

Therefore, the concept of a home equity loan was introduced by the finance industry, where a second loan is granted to the home owner, if the first loan is lower than the value of the house. However, in case the homeowner defaults and the home is sold, the home mortgage or the first/primary loan is paid in the beginning and then from the remaining balance, the home equity loan is paid. Since the home equity loan has lower preference in the order of receiving the principal, it was deemed more risky and therefore it was expected that this home equity loan would be paying higher interest rates.

Reverse Mortgage:

Some older people who were no longer working, but owned a home, needed access to capital. These people could not take a loan and pay it back as they did not have sufficient income. Finance Industry realized that these people may simply be interested in getting regular payments from the equity of their homes and the lender could sell the home to recover the money, after these people pass away. This need of older people was fulfilled with the introduction of the concept of a reverse mortgage. This concept was first introduced in United States in 1960s. This need based concept has also been introduced to many emerging countries now. http://en.wikipedia.org/wiki/Reverse_mortgage

From Stock exchange to Dematerialized Shares:

The Dutch East India company was established in the year 1602 to do trading in East Asia (A similar company, the British East

India company was formed two years earlier in Britain). It was the first company to issue stocks and also was involved in setting up the first stock exchange in the world, the Amsterdam Stock Exchange, for trading in the stocks and bonds. For a long time, shares were issued and traded in physical paper form. As volumes grew, the concept of a separate organization called clearing organization became popular to settle trades between the buyers and the sellers. The brokers of buyers and sellers used to bring physical share certificates to the clearing organization's office. The clearing organization worked to verify and exchange the shares among the buyers and sellers.

With advances in technology and omnipresence of personal computers in 1980s, computers were utilized for trading process. In order to make the process more efficient, the concept of dematerializing of shares was introduced where physical shares were destroyed and instead an electronic record was created in a depository organization. With this the exchange of shares could be done electronically. This process was faster and cheaper than the paper based process. This was possible due to the advances in information technology where customers could access electronic accounts from their places.

While these innovations of electronic trading and setting of transactions on computers was done by utilizing the new technologies, introducing these processes also needed an understanding of the customer's psyche that the customer would trust an electronic record and would not need a physical paper based share certificate.

Emerging countries started utilizing electronic trading only in the 1990s and the electronic settlement using dematerialized shares became popular only in the 2000s.

Derivatives:

A number of customers wanted to have an option of either purchasing or selling of an underlying asset at a later date at a pre-determined price. This asset could be a financial asset like a share of a company or a real asset like oil or a commodity. This led to the creation of derivatives, financial instruments which represent a contract between a buyer and seller to perform a transaction at a later date, under certain conditions. The derivative could be an option, future, a forward or a hybrid contract. The value of payoff of the derivative is based on the underlying value of the assets. This is another financial product that needed understanding the customer's need and psyche, before it could be conceived.

Securities Lending and Broker Dealer systems:

While the western world started regulating their financial systems and the securities trading activities as early as 1930s, the developing world governments did not have the expertise and resources to do so till 1990s. As an example, United States formed the SEC (securities and exchange commission) in 1934 to overlook all financial trading activities, India formed a similar entity, SEBI (securities and exchange board of India) in 1992. In the same year, China also formed the China securities regulatory commission, which later in 1999 became an improvised authority by the 1999 China securities law.

The western world, however has moved on to even more innovation in the financial domain in the 1990s. Many organizations who had excess cash during good economic periods had invested the cash in securities issued by government organizations and other private sector corporations. During lean periods, these organizations had to sell these securities due to their need of cash.

However, many times these securities had to be sold at a loss due to sub-optimal market conditions at the time the organizations needed cash.

This need gave rise to the business of Broker Dealers. These organizations worked as intermediaries between Cash surplus companies who would lend money for short terms to other organizations and those that would utilize the securities owned by them for collateral purposes. With advances in electronics and computing, very large transactions are conducted by organizations like J P Morgan and the Bank of New York to facilitate such transactions. These companies are able to evaluate market value of securities being offered as collateral with the inputs of ratings agencies and then get money from lending companies against these securities. The securities are electronically locked at the clearing houses so that they cannot be sold by the borrowing company. With the 2008 recession, government has been regulating this business segment to curb overleveraging and over-risk taking by organizations.

Ratings Systems:

Customers trading financial assets needed to get an independent perspective about the financial instruments. On the other side, the companies selling these financial instruments realized that a positive statement about them from a third party would be helpful to them. This led to the concept of third party rating agencies, rating the companies and the individual financial instruments being sold. The third party rating agencies (like S&P, Moodys')charge a fees from the companies who they are rating. These rating agencies are fulfilling the need of both the parties and thrive due to the element of trust on them from both sides. These organizations have to maintain a high level of independent decisions and integrity to keep their brands and reputation.

Insurance Industry:

The need of modern insurance was created in the 17th century Britain due to cover the risks of the business houses utilizing ships that travelled to long distances. There was a small probability that one of the many cargoes and ships might not be able to reach the destination safely and create a huge loss to the business owner utilizing that ship. Though the potential loss was huge, the probability of this event was low. The mathematical theory of probability was utilized to distribute the potential loss to a large number of ships and cargos (a transposition methodology). A small amount of money "premium" was charged to a large number of business owners to insure them for a potential loss. This concept was then utilized for insuring homeowners against a loss by fire in UK and US. In later years, this concept has been applied to other assets to create numerous types of insurances like Auto Insurance, Life Insurance, Health Insurance, Travel Insurance etc. Now, almost every asset can be insured against a loss.

Within these insurances, they have utilized the concepts of addition methodology where multiple types of assets can be insured together. For example, a customer can purchase a Car Insurance to protect from theft of the car or damage to the car in an accident. Car Insurance can be purchased for a third-party liability arising from damage to some other person's property in case of an accident or a health care bill for another person suffering during a car accident. All these insurances could be bundled together and purchased as a part of one package of Car Insurance.

The concept of bundling together of multiple insurances has been utilized to create the concept of Private Client Insurance. Here, the combined insurance package is provided to a person for his home, cars, personal belongings like art, and any liability from certain court cases. The insured person is generally a person of high net worth who would like personal attention from the insurer, he is interested in saving money by getting a combined insurance policy. The insurance company also saves money as it does not have to utilize the services of multiple sales agents and departments to sell different insurances. Further, the insurance company charges a large premium for this combined insurance policy.

Micro Insurance:

The concept of micro-credit for poor people has been transpositioned to the Insurance domain to create the concept of a micro-insurance industry in many emerging economies. Here, smaller insurance companies insure poor people in a particular geography. The amount of insurance is small and therefore the premium charged is also very small. An example of micro-insurance is an insurance for $500 with the premium being charged as $5 per month. Many times, it is not possible for a large insurance company to utilize its resources for micro-insurance as it is a labour intensive work. Large insurance companies therefore tie up with small companies to provide micro-insurance in a small region. Micro-insurance is done based on certain guidelines of the government and the insurance regulatory organizations. The smaller insurance companies providing micro-insurance also get themselves re-insured from larger insurance companies.

During the great recession of 2008, the concept of credit default swap insurance came in the news. It is an insurance for a lending agency against default by a borrower of a loan. This insurance was abused by many financial institutions as the default risk was assumed to be very small for the calculations of the premium. When a large number of creditors defaulted due to the housing market collapse, it affected large financial companies and even the largest of American insurance companies. Mortgage backed assets had been bundled and sold to large investors and financial organization during the preceding housing boom which lasted till 2007. However, the underlying mortgages which composed these bundles, had turned bad as the borrowers of the home loans had stopped paying back their loans after the home prices had started falling down and interest rates had risen. Despite constant efforts for an year in 2008, the FED was forced to offer a $ 700 Billion plan to purchase the 'toxic-debt', a term for under-performing loans mostly mortgages in different forms. Also, the government realized that the size of the prime mortgages (a term for loans given to people with good credit histories) defaulting increased to a number higher than the sub-prime mortgages (a term given to people with sub-optimum credit ratings).

Perhaps, the underlying cause of the problem is what can be called a borrower's 'free put option'. A homebuyer in America gets a 'free put option' when he takes a mortgage. He can walk away from the property leaving it to the bank, as the collateral is the property itself and nothing else. Most state governments will not allow the banks to go after the home buyer's other assets or future income.

In the previous decline of real estate market, in the early 90s, borrowers displayed patience through the downturn and did not use these options, probably because their down-payment was higher at that time. In the 2000s, many home buyers purchased homes with 0% down payments and they had not much to lose if they walked away from the properties. As the decline in home prices continued in 2008, more homeowners – even those who could afford to make payments – had started using this "free put option", thereby increasing the size of the 'toxic-debt', creating a vicious cycle.

In a way, the Insurance industry grows due to its customers' insecurities and potential liabilities, and new insecurities of customers can be utilized to create new insurance products.

New type of Insurance need identified:

Many people in the US have their relatives, friends and acquaintances visiting them from abroad. As these relatives could fall sick and need medical care which is very expensive in USA, many people take the travelers' health insurance for their relatives. A recent change in law has created a new potential of liability for these customers. This new US law requires the sponsor of the VISA to assume any liability for "any public charge" which United States government may have to incur due to this visitor. Perhaps, the insurance industry needs to come up with an insurance to protect the sponsor of the visitor for any "public charge".

Leveraged Buy Out:

Henry Kravis, founder of KKR created a record when he bought RJR Nabisco in 1988 for $31 Billion. Mr Kravis paid the money to the shareholders of RJR Nabisco by taking debt from banks based on the assets and the ability of the company to pay back the loan. Essentially, KKR were able to convince lenders that the company has enough assets and income to pay back the loan. The concept of an LBO Industry is based on buying all the shares of the company by taking a debt on the basis of the assets of the firm. This is like mortgaging the property to buy the property, or in terms of innovation, an application of the home mortgage concept to a corporation to purchase the corporation. This concept of investing in equity of the company is similar to the concept of a Venture Capital investment which is done in a small early stage company.

Private Client :

A rise in the number of super rich millionaires globally since the 1990s has given a new customer segments to various financial companies to target. Financial companies cater to the needs of these individuals on a one to one basis. The generic name of financial products for this customer segment is called "Private Client", for example Private Client Banking, Private Client Insurance, Private Client Wealth Management. As the names may make it obvious to readers, Private Client Banking is the concept where the banker goes to the client's premises to cater to the client's banking needs rather than the usual scenario where a bank customer going to a retail division of a bank for his needs. Similarly, Private Client Insurance is offered by a few Insurance companies offering combined insurance policies for the client's home, office, cars, art collections and liability. Private client wealth management is the concept where the client allows a large amount of his financial assets like stocks, bonds and cash to be managed by a wealth management firm. The wealth management firm charges a fees which has a variable component based on the annual returns generated on the assets by the wealth management firm.

Euro, An innovation of having a common currency:

After the world war II, many countries adopted the principles of Keynesian economics which tilt towards socialistic policies. The governments created policies of protectionism to keep jobs at home and have industries to keep countries self-sufficient. Many countries like India and China which were important players in international trade before the 1940s, participated minimally in international trade by limiting both imports and exports. However, from 1980s, with the influence of world leaders like Margaret Thatcher and Ronald Reagan, the classical school of economics became popular and global trade started rising. After the end of soviet union, free global trade became a norm for most nations.

However, for global trade, US Dollar remained the primary global currency. With increased global trade, many smaller countries in Asia and Europe with floating exchange rates, faced severe impact on their currencies due to changes in current account (a term used for balance of payments between nations based on the imports and exports of goods).A currency going up against the dollar would make the export based industries uncompetitive whereas a currency going down against the dollar would make the oil and other imports expensive, thereby increasing internal inflation of the nation.

European nations, though individually small, realized that they could get together and make a large economic zone like United States. To trade in this European Union, a common currency, Euro was introduced to give a competition to United States Dollar as an international trading currency. Though a transposition methodology has been applied to create Euro, the underlying principles of a single currency economic zone are missing, as the individual nations have the freedom to make their own economic and political changes. With the recent crisis in many European countries like Greece and Spain, there is pressure on these European nations to reduce independence and consider impact on the European Union, while making policy changes.

INNOVATIONS IN THE WATCH INDUSTRY

The wrist watches evolved a hundred years ago from the Pocket Watches and started becoming popular in the 1920s. The wrist watch industry is unique that it has seen a wide range of changes in the design and technologies, utilizing multiple innovation techniques.

This industry has used techniques to increase efficiency, save costs, and utilized different set of materials to serve new segment of customers. Some customers use it simply as an instrument to tell time whereas others wear it like a jewelry.

Originally, the wrist watches were mechanical instruments with inbuilt spring-based-engines needing rotation of its key every day.

These watches were popular for more than half a century. In fact till the late 1970s, owning any watch was considered prestigious. It was one of the most popular gift item during important occasions like marriages and birth anniversary. Many developing countries like India were importing watches as they could not domestically produce enough number of watches. The quality of watches was a question those days, as some of the mechanical watches used to deteriorate in quality and precision after a couple of years.

Automatic watches were later introduced which did not need daily tightening of keys of the watch, instead the movement of the watch activated the engine. Many expensive watches like Rolex are still mechanical watches.

Japanese watch industry. utilized electronics to create digital watches and made them popular These digital watches utilize quartz movements and battery based power. These watches had better accuracy as well as lower prices. As these watches were both accurate as well as affordable, these soon became a rage among the masses. Many additional features were available in these watches like Calculators, Alarms and Calenders

The digital watches became very popular when they got introduced in the 1980s, but later their prices fell down drastically in the 1990s. In many Asian markets of HongKong and Singapore, the large whole-sale stores started selling these watches based on weight to smaller-retailers. However, sharp drop in prices have also downgraded the customers' 'feel-good factor' about possessing these watches. Wearing these cheap watches reflected poorly on the status of the person wearing it. Thus, many Customers moved back to wearing analog watches with traditional dial and an hour and a minute arm. A watch in the 1970s was considered a prized possession, but now the prices of most watches had become low and affordable by the mid 1990s. Realizing that some consumers want to use watches as status symbols, expensive watches like Rolex again came into prominence.

Many such companies are doing well selling these very expensive watches each selling for thousands of dollars. People buying these watches are not looking for an instrument to tell them time, but are looking for an instrument to tell others about their status and bank balance.

In the mid 1990s, there was a wide gap between the low end digital or mechanical watches and very high end automatic watches. Many Japanese companies realized this gap and introduced mid-range watches. In the last two decades, there has also been a market movement towards utilizing environment friendly products utilizing Green technologies. CITIZEN, riding on this wave, introduced a brand called 'Eco-drive' which is based on solar technology. These watches look like traditional dial-based mechanical watches, but use solar power. Price wise, these are mid range (cost range $$200-$800). These watches are riding on the market trends as described in the previous chapter on Consumer Psychology. Even though the customer has to pay hundreds of dollars more to get the solar technology in these watches, the customer is willing to pay for the sake of environment and carrying a symbol of Ecology friendly product. The owner of these Eco-drive watches does not need to replace the batteries of these watches. The picture below is of an eco-drive watch with night-glow, world time, stop watch timer and alarm besides the solar based charging.

However, a few cheaper versions of this watch were created by removing some of these features. One of the eco-drive watches does not have night-glow, does not have alarm, stop watch timer or world time. This one is much cheaper but carries a more traditional appeal.

(The picture above is a solar watch from CITIZEN with advanced features like world time, nightglow, stop watch etc. The picture below is of a plain solar watch design which costs much less but has a conservative appearance)

Global positioning technology has been utilized to create very expensive Atomic Watches. These watches receive radio signals from towers located around the world give them precise information about time. The selling point for these watches is that these watches will give accurate local time to the owner anywhere in the world. The manual of these watches is bulky as too many features have been loaded into these watches. However, expect them to be much simpler in the years to come as people prefer to use easy to use products and dislike excessively complex features. Many watches have add-on features like timers, chronographs and alarm functions and others have added functionality for heart-rate monitoring and time clocks.

Utilizing the transposition methodology, an e-Paper smartwatch "Pebble" has been lauched. Besides having a cool E-Paper display, it can also connect to your android phone or iPhone to run apps. Similarly, Sony has launched an android wristwatch that can pair with an android device. The iPod Nano, though not a watch, also allows utilizing a strap to use it like a watch.

Innovation has fueled the development of such a wide range of watches, and it is always a question for the watch company executive about what approach to take and how to further change the product.

INNOVATIONS IN IT INDUSTRY

IBM, the long time leader of IT Industry started in the nineteenth century as an organization to support government's census work. It utilized its technology to solve the problem of counting large numbers based on complex calculations and algorithms. It later developed solutions to help large organizations in managing their accounts and inventory. IBM also sent some of the first computers to Asia through the international branches of large multinational companies.

Flat Files to Relational Databases:

Till the late 1980s, most organizations were utilizing COBOL based application software programs. These programs used to run on mainframe servers. The technology of these mainframe machines was proprietary to a select large Computer companies like IBM, Unisys, Digital Equipment etc. For a COBOL based program, the data was stored in a text file in the form of line by line records. The various data elements were stored with fixed lengths either together or separated by spaces in a line. The COBOL program would then read the file line by line, segregate information based on field lengths, and would then process it as per the program's logic. The resulting data from computations would then either be printed on paper or would be stored in another file. The program writing process was not that complex but was long time taking. For example, if a date field had to be updated in the 5th row of a 1000 line document, each of the rows had to be read serially, and then re-written to a different file. The program would have the instructions that the data in the 5th row had to be read, segregated into various fields using fixed length size and then updated, before being written to the new file.

Larry Ellison from Oracle Corporation made the concept of a relational database system popular with his Oracle database in the 1980s. He utilized a research paper written in IBM on relational database systems to create this database. In a relational database system, the physical data is stored and managed by a database engine. The logical representation of the data is in a tabular format, and is displayed in a format as per the requirement of the user. The user would not need to know how the data is physically stored in the database. A new language SQL (Structured Query Language) became popular on Relational Database systems. The language had a simple syntax where the data elements to be queried could be specified in a few lines of code using the logical names of the data elements and the database engine would fetch that data from the physical storage and display it in a format required by the user. Unlike a COBOL based program, the user would not need to know the file name where the data is stored or the format in which the data is stored.

An SQL command is short and easy to understand and remember:

e.g. SELECT CUSTOMER_NUMBER, FIRST_NAME, LAST_NAME FROM CUSTOMER WHERE LAST_NAME='ELLISON';

This query would return the details of the customers whose last name is ELLISON.

And,

UPDATE CUSTOMER SET CUSTOMER_TEL='8005656890' WHERE CUSTOMER_NUMBER=2056;

This SQL command would would update the telephone number of the customer with customer_number of 2056.

In the first SQL command, the database engine fetches the customer's number, first name and the last name of all the customers whose last name is ELLISON. The Programmer does not need to know how is the data stored in the file on the disk, that task is managed by the database engine. In the second SQL statement, the database engine updates the telephone number of the customer where the customer number is 2056. Again, the programmer leaves the task of updating both the physical location of the data as well as the structure of the stored data to the database engine, which does it under the covers. To do either of these tasks in COBOL language, it would take the programmer to write around 100 lines of code and would usually take a day of work.

Business intelligence from data:

With faster access to multiple sources of data using SQL language, demand for data analysis also grew. The concept of storing large amounts of historical data from multiple sources and then analyzing it to find useful trends for business intelligence became popular in the late 1990s. Instead of the business managers of corporations asking the IT departments to generate routine reports to be used for analysis, business managers now wanted tools which they can utilize on their own to generate reports as per their requirements, at any time.

For analysis, it was required that data from disparate systems is brought together so that comprehensive analysis could be done. As data could be stored in different formats and sources like Oracle Databases, Sybase Databases, Mainframe computers, the first challenge was how to move data from different types of databases together at a single place, being called a "Data Warehouse".Also, some data would require transformation when moving from source to the data warehouse, for example a date field might be written as 'Jan-10-1985' in one system, '10/1/1985' in another and '1/10/85' in another system. This need was fulfilled by ETL tools, the ETL tools (Extraction Transformation and Loading) like IBM Datastage and Informatica Powercenter became popular in early 2000s for their power of connecting to the multiple operational databases simultaneously, transforming the data so that the data could be loaded in the data warehouse and then using techniques for very fast loading of the data in the data warehouse.

The second issue for business intelligence solutions in a data warehouse was the issue of analyzing the large amounts of data to solve the needs of the business. Many tools have been developed for this need to make data analysis easy for business managers. A few different techniques are utilized by these tools to make the task of analyzing relevant data easy for business users. These tools display business names for the database fields while displaying important information to the business users. Also, these tools summarize certain data that can be selected by the business users to generate useful business reports. Many of these tools pre-calculate the resulting data and store them in the database to give faster response to the business user. IBM's COGNOS has gone a step further by introducing the concept of a "Cube" where large pre-calculated values are stored in a text file in lieu of the database, which saves the retrieval time, by saving the overhead time of fetching data from the physical database and then transforming it to displaying in a logical format. As the data is retrieved from a text file and no calculation is required, the response to a user's request is almost instantaneous.

These business intelligence software tools have become popular since late 1990s to analyze corporate data to find trends for the business managers. These tools were utilized in many ways but were mainly used by Marketing managers to identify trends in various geographical regions.

SAS (Statistical Analysis System):

To enhance the learning experience of business managers in identifying these trends, the concept of statistical analysis was applied to business intelligence solutions. SAS (Statistical analysis system) is one of the most popular statistical analysis software used in business intelligence solutions. Besides the core feature of statistical analysis, it has other important features like ETL (Extraction Transformation and Loading) tool, Report generation and graphics to give a comprehensive data warehousing, business intelligence and forecasting solution for business managers. Generating Statistical analysis on data is one thing, but analyzing it is another. While tools like SAS are able to do statistical analysis and generate reports, analyzing the statistical output requires specialized skills. Many organizations are now hiring trained professionals in statistics to understand these statistical reports and relate it to the business requirements. Though statistical analysis has gained popularity in organizations for business strategy work, it is not without shortcomings. The results of statistical analysis can be modified based on the data sample being used, the size of the sample data being used, the variables being used to run the regression analysis and choosing the dependent variable.

ERP Solutions - Reusing pre-written code:

In lieu of writing new code for automating routine business functions, ERP solutions (from companies like SAP, Peoplesoft/Oracle) provide an option of reusing pre-written code for these business functions. These software solutions have software packages for standard business functions like Finance/Accounting, Human Resources, Manufacturing processes, Supply chain management, Project Management and Customer relationship management. The functionality can be customized and extended as per the unique requirements of a particular company. Customizing and implementing these functions with ERP solutions is faster and it is easier to maintain than writing fresh code from start as the pre-written code is standardized. These software solutions also utilize logic based on government regulations and best practices which is helpful to the senior management in for compliance.

Previous to arrival of ERP solutions, the software pieces were developed individually by different departments and it was difficult to combine and standardize the data and functional flow. However, ERP standardized the storage and data flow processes.

Infrastructure architecture:

From the early to mid 1990s, the concept of a client server architecture became popular. The server was supposed to be a large back end computer doing calculations for business logic and manage the database servers, whereas the client was the personal computer of the user which would have the software to display data in a user friendly and interactive manner. Many software solutions like Power builder and Oracle Forms 4.5 were installed on the personal computer of the user. Software was written utilizing these software products to make the use of software very user friendly. These solutions would fetch the data from back end servers, generally larger computers in the IT centers of corporations over the corporate LAN (Local Area Networks). The servers would do the huge number crunching and coordination of the data changes among multiple users. Though the software solutions became easy to use for end users due to these front-end heavy software products, the maintenance task became complex and time consuming for the software developers. Each time a change was to be implemented, it was not only to be updated in the back end server, it was also required to be updated in the personal computer of the users. As the number of personal computers with client software was equal to the number of users, many times a small change in the software solution had to be implemented in thousands of personal computers.

After mid 1990s, internet use in United States and the world exploded. Internet browsers like Netscape and Internet explorer became popular tools for most computer users. This gave rise to the concept of a thin-client. A thin-client was an internet browser used for displaying the web pages for an application to the users. The processing for the program logic remained in the back end server. To host the web pages, a web server hosting web pages became part of standard software infrastructure.

However, this configuration also had a particular weakness. The HTML technology for web pages was primarily a display mechanism for static pages and could not support providing complex business logic. Here, the web pages could be used for display of static pages and the back end database servers were used for database calculations, and the business logic had to be built within the database servers using procedural languages like PL/SQL. This tied up an application to a particular database system and made it difficult to switch to another database at a later time.

The IT Industry realized this gap, and created an application server. An application server software (like IBM Websphere and Weblogic) is the middle tier sitting between the front end web server and the back end database servers. This application server is a software engine where complex business logic could be written using java programs and deployed in the engine. The engine has the capabilities of scaling up to handle thousands and sometimes millions of simultaneous transactions and users. There are multiple ways this could be done: either by increasing the capacity of an application server or having multiple application servers to work simultaneously. For the first approach, one could create an application server with more memory and utilize a higher capacity processor. For the second approach, you could get multiple application servers some on the same physical server and some on other physical servers to work together. To ensure that workload is distributed among these many application servers, a load balancer is utilized. A load balancer routes web based user requests among the many web and application servers. Initially this routing was done on a round robin basis. Unfortunately, round robin mechanism had an issue: a complex business application has a series of interactive steps done in the application server engine. If the series of steps do not happen at the same application server, the process logic at a later step would not have information about a prior step. This gap was identified and the concept of session-affinity was introduced at the load balancer level. With session-affinity, all requests from a particular user would always be routed to the same web and application server from the load-balancer.

A web based user request comes to the load balancer, and the load balancer routes it to the multiple web and application servers, while maintaining session affinity for each user. This system is scalable and efficient. What could go wrong now? What will happen if one of the application servers gets shut down either due to a technical glitch, excessive overload or for doing scheduled maintenance. The load balancer would keep sending the request from a particular user to the same web and application server and as the application server is shut down, the user request would fail. In order to fix this issue with the IT Infrastructure, the concept of session persistence was introduced. Here, the details of all users' sessions were synchronized among multiple application servers.

A user session has information about the multiple steps that a user has taken during the course of an application. Once this information is available to all application servers, there would be no issue even if the user request is passed on to a different application server.

Messaging Systems:

While this multi-tier architecture composed of a load balancer, web and application servers and database layer was being utilized in the first decade of 2000s to create new computer based applications, many older organizations still had important applications running on mainframes and other older technologies. Organization realized that rewriting these applications with new technologies would be time taking and expensive. Some computer scientists suggested that may be these older systems could be retained but a link may be established between the newer technology based systems and these older systems. A messaging server filled this need. A messaging server is utilized to pass messages between multiple systems in a way that the messages do not get lost and IBM's Websphere MQ is a dominant player in this business.

Hibernate to Data warehouse:

In Relational databases, data was organized in a normalized form - for easier access and update operations. When data is organized in a normalized form, the program logic to retrieve data requires joining data stored in multiple tables, or data stored in a tabular form. Information is stored in such a way that data is segregated and same data is not kept in more than one place. Later, for Business intelligence projects where data from multiple sources had to be aggregated and analysis had to be done on it, it required that the data may be repeated at one place for the sake of easier and faster access. The data was de-normalized (for OLAP) for faster reading and data mining purposes.

Programming language like Java and Dot net contained the business logic but still had to rely on databases engines for storing data in a normalized or denormalized way. Java Programmers had to rely on the experience of database experts for database designing. However, Hibernate software changed this scenario as data could be stored and self-managed by a middle tier engine sitting between the Java-engine tier and database tier. Hibernate software organizes data in an object-oriented-structure. With Hibernate, a java programmer does not need to take the help of database experts for designing data in the database.

This type of Object-Oriented-structured data is difficult for traditional database designers to understand, as the data is neither normalized nor de-normalized. This has now created a need for a a tool which can convert Hibernate based data to either normalized or de-normalized data to be used with traditional business intelligence tools. Alternatively, new business intelligence tools are needed which can understand this Object-Oriented-structure data.

DOT COMs and INNOVATION:

Internet has become a platform for easy distribution of software like music, movies, pictures and data. The data could be of many forms like information, news and personal content. Internet has also been used as a medium to advertise and sell various products and help people make friends and do social networking. Internet has been used to share ideas and thoughts and also to get opinions from others in forms of surveys.

Due to the nature of many products which require the customer to touch and feel them before purchasing them, not every can be sold on internet. But many things can be sold on internet, particularly standardized items and those items that can be bought without physically touching them.

Though unlimited number of examples of internet based companies are there, a few interesting Venture Capital Funded companies and the innovation frameworks being used by them are presented here:

Partsearch Technologies (PARTSTORE.COM):

One day in 2006, a plastic part in our Home dishwasher got broken. This was a small rolling wheel on which the tray slides. Without this part, almost one half of the dishwasher was inoperative.

Since we had the yearly appliance repair service contract with our utility company, I called the utility company's service center to fix this dishwasher. The technician came to our house promptly but told us that the dishwasher is more than 25 years old and he does not have spare parts for such an old dishwasher. He also gave compliments about this old dishwasher and said this dishwasher is more rugged and superior compared to the newer models. At this point, I had started contemplating replacing this dishwasher but it would have cost me nearly a thousand dollars to purchase it and get it installed.

A random Google search brought me to Partstore.com, where I was surprised to see a large collection of obscure parts of appliances and electronics. The web site was so user friendly, it had the detailed design of my dishwasher along with the names and part numbers of each part. Using the diagram, I found the part number and ordered it on partstore.com. It cost me only $7 to get this part home, installation was done free of cost due to the maintenance service contract.

This company, Partsearch technologies has compiled an online catalogue of more than 8 million spare parts for electronics, appliances and other items. It does not store the parts but has developed a supply chain system management to get the parts from the vendors who sell these.

The company is now part of the Best Buy Group.

Diapers.com:

Vinit Bharara and Marc Lore, the founders of Diapers.com realized that any product which the customer does not need to physically touch before purchasing can be sold successfully on the internet.

Things such as Clothes and Shoes are difficult to sell as the customer wants to try them on before purchasing. A product like Diaper for children are bought in bulk by parents based on the size. There are only a few popular companies selling these and the primary concern while purchasing Diapers is price and timely delivery.

Vinit Bharara and Marc Lore started the company in 2005 selling diapers and later added a few other baby products like baby milk.

Both of them developed an efficient algorithm for supply chain management to deliver products on time at competitive prices. The company became successful and was sold to Amazon.com for $540 million in 2010, just five years after the start.

Dollarshaveclub.com:

This internet company provides a monthly supply of shaving blades to people for as less as a Dollar a month. Dollarshaveclub.com is modeled after companies like Diapers.com where a single product is being sold at highly competitive prices, owing to economies of scale and cutting out most of the middle layers between the manufacturers and the consumers.

Xobni.com :

Xobni (spells reverse of Inbox) is a product utilized for indexing and searching hundreds of thousands of mails of users. Most email servers organize emails based on date, but Xobni allows the user to organize emails as per email sender and conversation thread. It also makes it easier for the users to search a relevant email due to its search and indexing capability. Xobni uses alternate route process methodology as the same function of organizing the emails and searching the mails is done using a different route. Xobni has a first mover advantage now, but major email providers like Yahoo, Gmail and Hotmail might utilize similar functionality later.

Surveymonkey.com:

Surveymonkey.com is an online survey tool. It allows users to get opinion from other online users. It is free up to 10 questions per survey and 100 responses per survey, but requires users to pay fees for reaching larger number of audience and getting response to a large number of questions. Another competitor to this website is GoPollGo.com which utilizes some features from social networking where people can do real time discussions. Both of these web sites save customers time and provide analytics based on customer segmentation and geography.

Zoomin.com:

The website allows users to aggregate their digital pictures from multiple web sites to this web site and sells add on features like printing pictures on Calenders, postcards, T-shirts and Mugs for a fees. The website uses the internet based medium to store the pictures, a transposition methodology and then adds features of printing pictures on physical objects for a fee.

Yummly.com:

Yummly is an aggregation web site used for the food recipes. It gathers information from multiple web sites like facebook about different recipes, it allows the user to filter foods based on various parameters like his nutritional requirements, diet, allergy and price.

Yapta.com:

Yapta.com has dared to enter the crowded business of online airline reservation. To compete in this tough business, Yapta.com not only offers the best fares available before a user books his ticket, but also ensures that if the prices are dropped later, a refund would be given to the customer from the airline. The website has added the functionality of returning the difference of fare due to reduction in fare.

Warby Parker.com:

Internet has enabled price competitiveness in sale of many "standard" articles like books, computer parts and electronics. However, it has not been able to do so for the "wearables" like clothes, shoes and glasses etc. Customers do not feel comfortable purchasing things before trying them on. Warby Parker realized this gap and has attempted to sell prescription glasses on internet. The web site has detailed instruction on choosing the size of the frame and sends upto 10 frames by mail. The customer can try the different frames and decide the one he wants to use. The company would then make the prescription glasses as per the doctor's prescription in the frame chosen by the customer and would then mail it to the customer. As the company does not have to pay for expensive retail outlets and there is an economy of scale involved, the glasses can be purchased at a cheaper cost than the retail store.

Hotwire.com:

A late entrant into the travel industry portals, Hotwire almost guarantees the lowest prices for hotels and car rentals. However, it does not tell the name of the Car Rental company or the name of the Hotel, before the customer makes a purchase. Also, many times the bookings done on Hotwire.com are not cancellable. The Rental Car companies and Hotels try to maximize their sales by offering very low prices on Hotwire.com and still hide their names until the customer has actually done the purchase. On a competing website like Hotels.com, the customer would probably have to pay slightly higher price, but would be able to know the name, details and pictures of the hotel, before making a booking.

7

TESTS AND EXAMPLES

· ·

*A*fter developing skills in identifying the various patterns of innovation frameworks in the objects around him, the reader needs to apply this knowledge to build new products and services. In this chapter, a few questions are posed to the reader about certain situations. The reader should ponder over what he/she would do and use the different innovation frameworks he learnt earlier to come up with solutions. The author's responses are given later for each of these. For best learning experience, the reader should write his thoughts in the blank spaces here before reading the author's response. Though the answers of the reader may be different from the author's responses, this exercise helps the reader learn different approaches to creating an innovative solution using the previously described frameworks.

1 What could be improved in a plastic water bottle?

_____

_____

_____

_____

_____

_____

2 How do I improvise on a DVD?

_____

_____

_____

_____

_____

_____

3 How can we use technology for Corporate Governance and ensuring that CEO do not de-fraud shareholders?

_____

_____

_____

_____

_____

_____

4 For 26/11/2008 MUMBAI TERRORIST ATTACKS: What technology Indian police could have used to catch all terrorists alive?

_____

_____

_____

_____

_____

_____

5 PHONES: LANDLINES, MOBILE PHONES AND INTERNET PHONES. I am running around the house taking phone calls from these. What can be done about it?

_____

_____

_____

_____

_____

_____

6 How can we green the home cooling process in summers to save energy costs in lieu of using an Air Conditioner?

_____

_____

_____

_____

_____

7 What can be improved in Email Services?

_____

_____

_____

_____

_____

8 How can we make Mobile Commerce easier to use?

_____

_____

_____

_____

_____

_____

9 How can we make a Domino's of Indian Food?

_____

_____

_____

_____

_____

_____

10 Can we improve the American Home Radiators and heating systems?

_____

_____

_____

_____

_____

_____

11 How can we protect eyes from extreme weather conditions?

_____

_____

_____

_____

_____

_____

12 What can I do so that I can shave my own head?

_____

_____

_____

_____

_____

13 What would you improve in modern toilets today?

_____

_____

_____

_____

_____

14 What would you like to improve in the mobile phone today?

_____

_____

_____

_____

_____

15 HOW WILL YOU MAKE A SUPER FUEL EFFICIENT CAR?

_____

_____

_____

_____

_____

_____

16 How to reduce cost of generating Solar Power?

_____

_____

_____

_____

_____

17 What needs to be improved in electric vehicles?

_____

_____

_____

_____

_____

18 How to create a new flavored soft drink.

_____

_____

_____

_____

_____

_____

19 What do we need to improve in the home based water filtering/treatment solutions

_____

_____

_____

_____

_____

_____

20 How to design a flush free toilet

_____

_____

_____

_____

_____

1. What could be improved in a plastic water bottle?

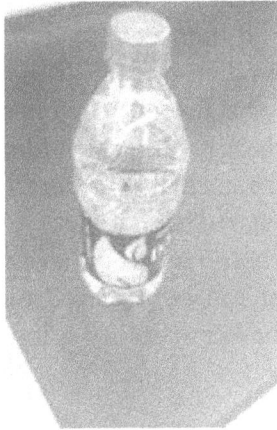

Commodity products like bottled water have fierce competition. Besides taste, quality and nutrients, packaging plays an important role in the brand positioning of such products.

The one liter and a half a liter plastic bottle for water has been around for many years, along with bigger and smaller versions. However, these bottle designs miss a few things:

For the 1 liter version, either you have to drink the full bottle during a short time or the water becomes warm after opening it, so you do not feel like drinking it later, specially the next day onwards. You can buy the smaller versions of this bottle and carry them in your car easily. However, if you are traveling by public transportation, you have to manage carrying many of these, which feels cumbersome and is not sleak.

If you have a 1 or a 2 liter bottle while you are traveling with friends/family, it is difficult to share the water unless you have glasses. One more issue is that you are forced to gulp the water from the bottle, instead of sipping it , which you could do if the bottle had a built in straw.

An alternate design for this bottle could be a small (half pint sized or smaller) bottle, with a modified base which allows another similar sized bottle to be connected to it. This could be achieved by putting grooves/threading on top of the plastic cap to screw/connect the bottle to the bottom of this modified bottle base. Connecting 3 to 4 of these together would make it easy and sleak to carry. It would keep each unit separate from the remaining ones, water could be shared with friends easily, and would keep the water fresh(since all bottles do not have to be opened).Another degree of improvement can be achieved by changing the design so that the water can be kept cool for a long time. Will leave this question for the reader ..

2. How do I improvise on a DVD?

I have been throwing away my old movie DVDs recently. Not because I do not like these old movies, but because these old DVDs collect dust and marks and start affecting the lens of the DVD player.

However hard one tries, the DVDs would go bad at the slightest level of mishandling or would start impacting the DVD player. The video cassettes /tapes for VCRs had a nice plastic cover where the tape would be hidden from all pollution and would be uncovered only after the tape is inserted in the VCR. However, the DVDs are open and ready to attract dust and scratches at the first opportunity. I wish some company recognizes this and starts creating DVDs with plastic covers, along with DVD players, so that the DVD gets exposed only after being inserted in the player.

Ideally, if one can buy a DVD of today and insert it in the jacket to be used with this new DVD player, this could become popular. Ditto would work for the camcorders with DVDs.

Alternately, once the price of read-only USB based flash drives go down, these could be used for selling media. In today's scenario, a machine with hundreds of usb-drive slots where customers insert thier flash drives and download media for a charge could be of some use.

3. How can we use technology to improve corporate governance?

A 2008 news in India conveyed that a leading IT company (Satyam) announced its plans of acquiring a money-losing real estate company owned by the promoter's family and it created waves of questions about corporate governance in India. A few months later, it was revealed that the CEO had defrauded the shareholders and brought the company close to bankruptcy. Many similar scandals have happened in United States in like the one in TYCO and ENRON.

It is known that promoters/managers have been taking the rest of the shareholders for a ride during board decisions, most of the times by using the 'independent' board members.

Numerous times, the managers have been not disclosing the full agenda before the board meeting and have sometimes even manipulated the minutes of the board meeting as per their own requirements.

An electronic solution where all shareholders can access and vote for a board agenda before the board meeting in a secure way could be helpful to organizations.

A weighted average of shareholders' opinion once accessible to the board would put an onus on the board members to take more responsible decisions

4. For 26/11/2008 Mumbai terrorist attacks: What technology could the Indian police use to catch the terrorists alive?

A family friend works for the special cell of Police in India, involved in fighting with terrorists and underworld. I talked to him about the terrorist attacks at the Taj Hotel on 26 Nov 2008 and asked him if they could have used some gas to make all people inside the hotel unconscious, thus making it much faster to catch the terrorists and rescue the hostages. He conveyed that the police does not use any such gases; though there are chemical gases like Chloroform, Carbon monoxide, Methane which can make people unconscious, these gases can kill people with their overdose. A gas which would instantly knock-down people by making them drowsy/unconscious, in a medically safe manner could be useful in such operations.

5. PHONES: Landlines, Mobiles and Internet phones, what can we do to make life easy?

I still need the following phones at my home: a fixed internet phone from my internet service provider, a usb drive based internet phone from magicjack which I carry with me when I travel, my cellular phone and an intercom phone for the building security and other residents to contact us. I have not mentioned our landline and my family's other cellular phones here.

Altogether, these are a lot of phones and sometimes we have to run around between the different rooms to reach these as we hear a ring. A cordless / blue-tooth protocol and equipment to receive calls from many of these to one phone device would probably be helpful.

6. How to save energy costs from home cooling in summers, in lieu of using an air conditioner?

When you ask for water in a United States restaurant, they serve it chilled, usually with ice. However, in Asia and some places in Europe, they ask you if you want the water at room temperature or cold.

Similarly, the cooling temperature at which people set their air-conditioners also changes from Individual to Individual. I like to keep it at 29 C, whereas some of my friends like it at 20-24 C.

This conveys the requirements for convenience change from person to person.

In India, people have been using earthen pots, like the picture I am attaching here for cooling water. It works on the principle of water evaporating from the pores of the earthen pot utilizing latent heat and making the remaining water cooler. In fact the higher is the outside temperature, the lower is the temperature of water in the earthen pot. My family prefers to use drinking water from an earthen pot, rather than from the refrigerator, as the temperature of water from it is much cooler than the tap water but warmer than the refrigerator water.

The electricity which is used in traditional air-conditioning systems is three to four times higher than the electricity being used by desert coolers or evaporative coolers.

These evaporative air cooling systems work on the basis of air being forced through wet evaporative pads. Due to the latent heat being utilized for partial evaporation of water in the pads, it makes the air passing through the water-soaked pads very cool. However, the humidity of the water goes up in the process and therefore these systems can be used only in relatively dry places and weather.

In order to reduce the humidity, 2 stage air-cooling systems have been recommended. Though I have seen many single stage air-cooler systems, I am yet to come across any installation of a 2 stage air-cooler system. Here the air being forced through water-soaked pads, is first pre-cooled through a heat exchanger thus reducing the moisture carrying capacity of the air.

However, these 2 stage air-cooler systems still produce air with 50-70% humidity.

While thinking about how to make an efficient condensing process/reducing the moisture-holding capacity of air while still keeping the electricity requirements low, I came across the idea of a a marriage of the water-cooling earthen pot systems with the 2 stage air-cooling systems.

Essentially, the heat-exchanger system could utilize the cool water from a Large earthen material Tank in the first stage of the 2 stage air cooling systems.

This design may become popular to cost conscious people in the developing world.

7. What can be improved in email services?

REGISTER IT:

Nearly 30 years after PCs started becoming popular, paper still rules the corporate world. With 'green' becoming popular and fashionable, something could be done to reduce the paper work. Some organizations/people print agreement documents, sign, then scan and send it as an email attachment. The receiver also goes through the same process.

IT guidelines from some government organizations and world bank require biometric authentication for document approval from officers.

Due to people leaving the organizations and their email accounts getting deleted, an exchange of email between organizations is still not considered good enough, though it has been approved legally in most countries.

A third-party service providing a secure place to save the electronic documents exchanged between organizations would be useful in reducing the paperwork between them.

It could be done with this proposed protocol:

- All organizations agree to a common box for cc of emails eg: ccbox@us.xyz.com

- All internal employees' emails and their managers' emails are arranged in a hierarchy. An automated process forwards emails received on ccbox with a copy to a particular employee to that employee's manager.

- Company A's officer sends an email to Company B's officer with a copy to the registered email service provider eg: regmail@regmail.com

- The regmail@regmail.com creates a unique mail # for the mail and forwards the mail with the unique mail # to the sender, receiver and the ccbox@companyA.com and ccbox@companyB.com.

- The automated process running on ccbox email id in each company forwards that email to the employee's managers.

The registered mail service would make money firstly by putting banner ads at the bottom of these emails, and secondly by charging cash in case any company wants a copy of the email to be presented in a legal dispute from the registered email service company.

HIGHER PRIVACY: After GMAIL, all other internet based email service providers have now started profiling users based on the emails they are sending and receiving. Many users would be willing to pay to an email service which does not profile their email content and ensures that it is deleted safely, so that users privacy is protected.

JUNK MAIL: While Junk mail is a headache for consumers, there could be ways of creating cash for consumers using Junk Mail. I first got this concept from the website http://www.freeride.com in the 1990s, when registered users were getting cash for clicking on advertisement banners on this web site. The same concept can be used in a new email service where users are paid points for browsing junk mails, that is paid by the corporate sponsors.

Frameworks Used: Transposition and Addition

8. How can we make Mobile Commerce easier to use?

Besides the ability to carry your mobile phone across the countries, the process for a mobile commerce transaction needs to be much easier than what it is currently.

Currently, you have to send a text message to a particular shortcode. For example, you send a text message/SMS with details of the merchant code and $ amount.

Thereafter a few more steps are required to confirm the transaction.

However, the process should be much easier for eg pointing your phone's camera (used as a reader) to the BarCode chart of the merchant, and pressing an authorization code and amount on the phone.

Or it could use the bluetooth capabilities of the phone to identify the merchant's bluetooth equipment connected to a wired network, and paying directly - rather than through the text messages/SMS.

9. Can we make a Domino's of Indian Food:

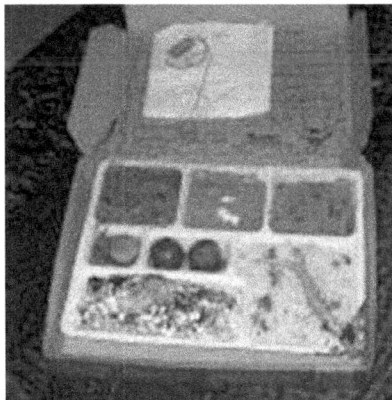

I came across a unique and stylish Food Pack in Ahmedabad, India. It is delivered by a popular local restaurant chain. The Food Pack is in Domino's style Cardboard box. It is a pack of 2 Paratha breads, Rice, 3 Side dishes, One lentil, dessert (warm Gulab Jamun) and pickles packed nicely in a silver foil.

There was also a plastic spoon and some after-food 'mukhwas'. The Food was very tasty and remained warm nearly 2 hours after it was packed.

The food was delivered within 30 minutes after I called the restaurant. The price was very reasonable (less than $$2 per box). This pack solved the major issue of finding quality Indian food, in right quantity, prepared and packed in a hygenic way, supported by a known brand, delivered to your doorstep in 30 minutes and another alternative to Pizza on Friday nights. The concept looks very attractive - with right execution and management - it could be used for the making of a Domino's of Indian Cuisine.

Frameworks: Transposition of the Fast Food Delivery with Indian food product

10. Can we improve the American Home Radiators and Heating systems:

A few years back in New Jersey, I was living in a rented apartment in Weehawken, NJ. One night, I woke up to change the temperature control setting in the device situated in the living room. I noticed that if I set the temperature in the living room to 60° F, my bed room temperature became 64° F, but when I set the living room temperature to 62° F, the temperature in the bed room went to more than 70° F, which was uncomfortable. (Ideally, I like the temperature to be 68° F.)

This is because the radiator's size in the living room is the same as the radiator's size in the bedroom, while the size of the living room is more than two times the size of the bedrooms.

While 62° F was not warm enough for the living room, the temperature in the bed room become uncomfortably hot.

During the day, if the living room temperature was set to 68° F, the bed room temperature became unbearably hot and we either sometimes shut down the valve to the radiator, or open the windows slightly.

Most American homes are heated with indirect heating through radiators. Hot water or steam comes to the radiators from the water boiler, usually located in the basement. These homes are single heating zones controlled by a single thermostat/temperature control device, mostly located in the living room.

The radiator sizes in the home can be changed to keep the temperatures in all rooms more or less the same. However, that would still mean loosing energy costs to keep the living room warm enough in the night , when it is not being used.

Probably, there is a big market to replace the existing heating systems with systems that can save energy costs by keeping the rooms not being used at slightly lower temperatures.

Frameworks Used: To develop the product requires an obvious need and uses the concept of Addition.

11. How can we protect eyes from extreme weather conditions?

Some days in New York's Winter, the temperature goes below 20 degrees F and cold wind is blowing fiercely. You want to stay inside, but still are forced to walk, specially in a city like New York.

Most people wear 4 layers of upper body clothing, 2-3 layers of lower body clothing and may be one or two layers on their head. Some people even resort to wearing monkey caps to cover their face.

But what about the eyes? Cold dry air touches the eyes and gives teary and red eyes to many people.

A normal pair of goggles has too much gap on the sides and does not protect the eyes enough.

A pair of Swimming goggles could have been a solution except for the fact that it has to be tied on the back of your head, is too tight on the eyes and looks odd.

Another solution could have been a set of ski-goggles as it has a foam rim to protect the sides, but it has also to be tied on the back and looks too big to look normal in a city.

A third option I identified as suitable and bought are the extra-sized UV-protection goggles made to cover and wear over spectacles. These are only slightly bigger than spectacles and cover the sides.

These could have been perfect, if only the glasses were non colored/clear and the rims had a thin foam cover, like the ski-goggles to cover the cold air from the sides.

12. What can I do so that I can shave my own head?

The owner of HeadBlade solved the answer by creating this toy-car like device which can be made to run on the shape of the head while cutting the hair. This device is like a car toy and it has wheels on one side. It can slide on all contours of the shape of the head like a car and in the process cuts hair with the shaving blade attached under it.

The product became an instant success in United States

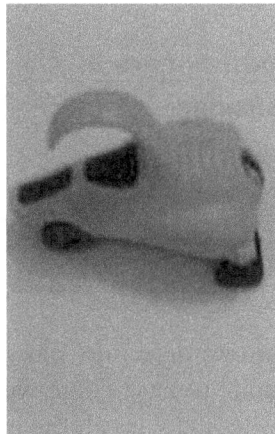

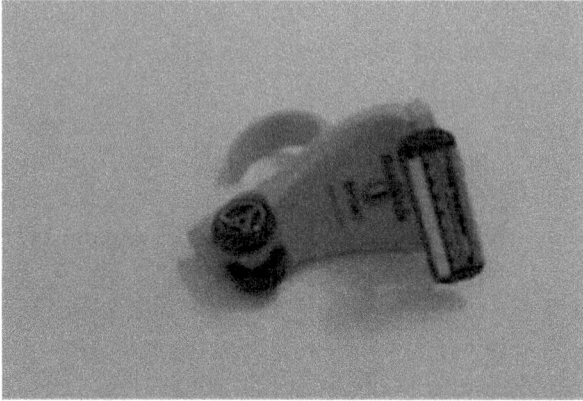

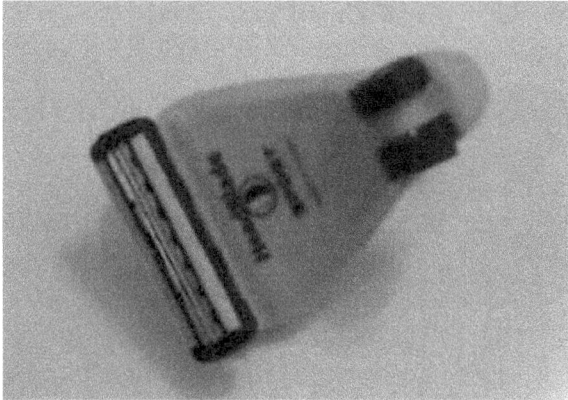

13. What would you improve in modern toilets today?

Electronic Sensor If It Does Not Flush Properly:

A few years back, sensory detection based flush systems were introduced in men's public toilets. These were introduced so that people do not have to physically touch the previous manual based flush systems. These systems were appreciated as they removed the risk of catching infection from touching the lever device of the manual flush system.

However, many men have faced a new situation in a public toilet. After a person uses the toilet, it is supposed to flush due to sensory detector. However, in many public toilets, the movement detector is not efficient: It either does not flush after the last person has used it or does not flush enough. To solve this problem, I noticed that some newer products have a manual flush option also, just in case somebody needs.

Perhaps an even better option would be introduce a foot pedal based activation system which may not even require a sensory detection system.

"Dual Flush" Water Tanks For Water Conservation:

In many emerging countries with scarcity of water, a dual flush water tank system has started becoming popular for use in toilets. This dual flush water tank allows the user to choose between

1.1 Gallons and 1.6 Gallons per flush, based on the need of the user. This system has not yet become popular in United States, as the water scarcity is still not a major issue in the US.

14. What Would You Like To Improve In The Mobile Phone Today?

Mobile Phones have added many features like FM Radio, Touch-sensitive screens, Internet browsers, games and personal laptop like capabilities. These could be improved and new software features added.

However, one of the most important need people have is to keep re-charging the batteries of these mobile phones. May be solar power concept can be taken from Citizen Eco-Drive watches, and utilized to design mobile phones which get charged by Solar and other light sources.

15. How Will You Make A Super Fuel Efficient Car?

Aptera Motors: Do you really need the fourth wheel?

During recessions or periods of high oil prices, fuel efficiency becomes an important concern for car buyers.

For many decades, car companies have been trying to make more fuel efficient engines or making engines utilizing cheaper fuels. Some important innovations have been done by companies making LPG kits and CNG kits to make cars use less expensive fuels. One of the most important innovations has been the creation of hybrid engines. Cars with hybrid engines store excessive energy created during idling (when the car is not moving but the engine is running, or when the engine is producing more energy than required) as battery power. This energy is later utilized to run the car, usually on highways.

Aptera motors used the frameworks of innovation and identified the important factors making a car consume more fuel as:

1 Weight

2 Drag (a force caused by wind against the surface area of the car)

3 Engine efficiency

Aptera motors identified that most of the fuel is consumed due to weight of the car and drag force. It has made a car which is in the shape of a bird to utilize aerodynamics to reduce the drag force. Further, it has only a single wheel at the rear, again to match the shape of a bird. While most cars have engines in the front and the power is transmitted to the rear wheels, Aptera chose to keep the engines attached to the front wheels to save the wastage of energy during transmission to the rear wheels. Aptera ensured that the quality of the car is light but still strong to ensure that the passenger feels safe.

Unfortunately, despite some successes in moving towards the goal of producing vehicles giving 200 miles per gallon, the company had to stop its operations due to lack of funding.

16. How To Reduce Cost Of Generating Solar Power?

eSolar: Incremental innovation to make Solar power cost meaningful

Most Solar power products are based on photo-voltaic cells. These photo-voltaic cells utilize sunlight to generate electricity. Despite the technology being available for nearly a hundred years, these photo-voltaic cells have been expensive and inefficient to produce electricity.

For nearly a century, most Solar power companies have been trying to create a more efficient photo-voltaic cells.

However, a company eSolar.com utilized a different approach. It used the combination methodology of innovation and combined the traditional steam based turbine with solar energy based heat.

Instead of using photovoltaic cells, the company's has decided to use mirrors to send large amount of solar heat to a tower containing water. Water gets converted to steam which is fed to a turbine to produce electricity.

It has produced a product where it claims it is more efficient than even coal to produce electricity. It can produce 46 MW of power from its basic plant spread over 160 acres of land (45 MW would be enough for around 100 K people in a developing country or 50 K people in a developed country).

FRAMEWORKS: It is an excellent example of combination methodology of innovation.

17. What needs to be improved in Electric vehicles?

Electric Vehicles are desired by many people due to cost savings from expensive gasoline and for environmental reasons. Many people are even willing to pay extra money for the sake of these cost savings and environmental reasons. However, existing EVs take many hours to charge the vehicle. It makes the use of an EV possible only for short distances. People who purchase these vehicles generally put the vehicle on a charger overnight, and then utilize it for short distances within their town. Going for a long trip is not possible without long breaks.

Nissan identified this issue and is addressing it with a technology where the car can be charged in only 10 minutes. Nissan is now utilizing a capacitor made up of Tungsten Oxide and Vanadium Oxide instead of Carbon to improve power.

18. How To Create A New Flavored Drink:

Aerated drinks are not in fashion these days. Consumers are becoming health conscious and prefer juices and flavored milk products. I came across the health benefits of Goat milk as it has much higher calcium and minerals than cow milk. Goat milk is 4 times more expensive than cow milk in United States. Due to price, mass consumption of the product in place of cow milk may not start. However, flavored goat milk using chocolate, rose and mango might become popular among children, in lieu of aerated drinks.

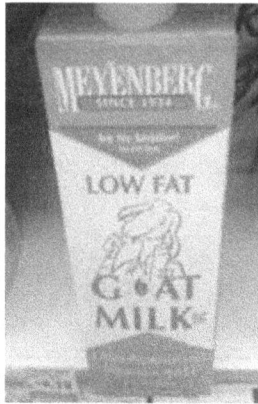

(attached below is the picture of the carton explaining
the benefits of Goat Milk)

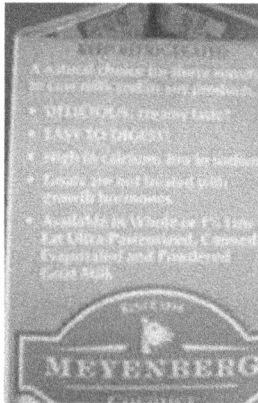

FRAMEWORKS USED: *This is an example of Alternate Means Methodology and Combination Methodology*

19. What do we improve in home water treatment/ filtering systems?

There are mainly two types of water treatment solutions popular:: Water Filtering and RO (Reverse Osmosis) machines. Water Filtering utilizes physical cleaning of the water from its impurities, whereas Reverse Osmosis systems reduces the hardness of the water by forcing water to move through a semi-permeable membrane. The issue with the current Reverse Osmosis process is that it may not remove the hardness in the water to an optimum level – it may reduce it to such a level that it even lacks the minimum minerals required for the human body.

I foresee future RO machines which will ensure the minimum minerals required for nutrition.

20. How to design a flush free toilet ?

Mr Bill Gates spoke to Indian news media in New Delhi recently and said "One of my ultimate dreams now is to reinvent the toilet - find a cheaper alternative to the flush toilet that does not require running water, has smell characteristics better than the flush toilet and is cheap.".

The material "LIQUIGLIDE" could be a key to creating such a toilet requiring no flush/water. Liquiglide is a structured liquid, it is rigid and can be applied like a solid, but has a surface like a liquid.

A coating of Liquiglide inside a plastic or glass container ensures that the surface becomes completely non-sticky. When it was applied inside a ketchup bottle, there was not even a drop of ketchup that could stay inside the bottle once the bottle was turned upside down.

(http://news.yahoo.com/blogs/technology-blog/mit-harvard-battle-create-life-changing-product-non-170117941.html)

8

INNOVATION FOR STRATEGY

· ·

Many management gurus have created strategy frameworks which sometimes are mutually exclusive and confusing to business leaders. While one strategy recommends ways of giving a strong competition to other players in the Industry, another one recommends co-operating and growing the pie of industry together. Coca Cola may be an example of the first type, where it works aggressively to crush any new entrant in the soft drinks business, where as many high technology companies are examples of the second type, where they work together to win new customers and provide a comprehensive solution to fulfill the customer's requirements.

Similarly, one strategy recommends diversifying into many fields to ensure consistent cash flows through business cycles, another one recommends focussing on core-competence and ignoring other business areas. While Mexico's billionaire Carlos Slim, with his more than a hundred diversified companies, could be used as an example of the first type of strategy, Microsoft's Bill Gates is an example of the second type with his prime focus on Microsoft's software products business.

During the 1990s, some management gurus recommended a strategy utilizing internet presence for all businesses, a few management gurus suggested against internet based businesses as internet businesses can face very high competition due to low barrier to entry. Now, in 2012 we can see successful business of both types – those that are primarily operating using internet and others that are still doing business traditionally with minimum utilization of internet. It appears that just when one is about to be convinced about one type of business strategy, he or she finds that an exactly opposite business strategy appears to be doing equally well somewhere else. So exactly what is a corporate strategy and how to decide which one will work for my business?

At a fundamental level, all Corporate Strategy is nothing but innovation(s) of business processes that can lead to higher profitability for an organization. Corporate strategy is a process innovation of alternate means where various means are employed for the end result of higher profitability. These Process innovations may lead to Product Innovations in some companies. While one type of process innovation works for one type of Industry, another type works for another type of Industry.

In this chapter, we will explore a few examples of the steps some leading industries and organizations have taken and will explain what process and product innovations these organizations have been doing to increase their profitability:

Strategy of Apple:

In the late 1990s, Microsoft's Windows had become the de-facto operating system for all personal computers and laptops. Apple's CEO Steve Jobs had realized that its Macintosh Systems which were being used primarily by the printing and graphics industry at that time, could not displace the Microsoft based personal computers and laptops in homes and offices. Apple decided to venture into new product areas to create a brand identity which appeals to the young customers. Apple started identifying the latest technologies and used transposition methodology to apply these technologies to existing products needed by customers to create new products. These products became popular for being the leading edge technology products and created a unique brand image for Apple. Almost all the technologies utilized by Apple were soon copied by other companies to come up with similar products later, but since Apple had the speed to keep itself ahead of others, the brand image continued to grow. Apple started utilizing combination methodology and transposition methodology to come up with newer products.

Apple first combined the digital storage technology to the concept of age old "Walkman" to create an iPod. Similar to the Sony Walkman of 1980s, this device was a small device and was used to listen to music while moving. It later added an LCD screen to this device so that customers can also look at the video along with listening to music. The instrument could also be utilized to watch movies. Young teenage followers wanted to be seen with the white earphones, an identification of iPod in early 2000s. Later, many similar products were launched by other companies, some at much cheaper prices providing digital music, but they could not get the media coverage and popularity as Apple had already built a brand image due to the first mover advantage and the rugged quality of its products.

Apple's next famous product was an iPhone. This product was created by combining the concept of a multi-use smartphone with the leading edge technology of a multi-touch screen. It had a finger touch screen made from scratch resistant glass. There were many previous smartphones (like HTC) which had a camera, a portable media device, an internet client, an email, a web browser, an SMS text facility, a Wi-Fi and 3G connectivity. iPhone combined all of these features but created a sturdier product and a more ergo-nomic interface by having a multi-touch larger screen with higher resolution. Further, it added an Application Store from where customers could install additional software products like GPS based Navigation system, a compass or games. These software products on the mobile phone vastly increased the usefulness of the operating system of this device.

Apple released its next product, an iPad, which was a tablet computer system. The product was released almost 10 years after the tablet released by Microsoft, but captured the whole market. This product became popular due to Apple's strong brand image, large number of features and a user friendly multi-touch interface. This product can be used to read books, watch movies, listen to music, browse the internet and use many other applications from Apple's store. The product utilizes combination methodology as it combines features from iPod and iPhone like finger touch screen, multi-touch display and features to listen to digital music, watch movies and browse the internet.

Constant race of technology product companies:

As we have seen from the rapid innovation by Apple, technology product companies have to always race against time to come up with new products with the latest in research and technologies. In a way, technology companies are always striving for First-Mover advantage. As newer technologies arrive, existing technologies get outdated. Companies like Sony and Apple grew into giant corporations with large brand equities because of their Chief Executives being in love with new technologies. Apple's Steve Jobs was able to utilize the latest technology available into his products and was able to come up with optimum products with good ergonomics. Similarly, Akio Morita, the founder of Sony was an engineer who loved new technology and was able to utilize new technologies to come up with ergonomic products like Tape Recorder, Pocket sized radio, Transistor based Television and the Walkman. The techno-zeal of founders of Apple and Sony is difficult to be replaced by Management professionals getting into the driving seats of technology companies after the founders leave their corporations. Management graduates have good skills in finance and business strategy, but the skills to grow technology companies are identifying new research work in technologies and use that work to create ergonomic and desirable technology products.

First User Advantage but at Optimum Time:

The touch screen technology on cellular phones was first made popular almost 10 years before Apple Launched iPhone. One of the first important products launched in this space were from a company Palm. Initially, Palm had launched a plastic stylus based touch screen where the user had to move the stylus on the screen at sharp angles resembling letters. The screen would decipher these movements as letters and store the words. However, there was a learning required to move the stylus in certain angles to resemble letters. Asking the user to learn using the tool is against the principles of ergonomics. In the later versions of smart phones, this was replaced by a flipping Qwerty keyboard as well as a touch screen based keyboard. As the touch screen was based on applying pressure, the user had to press harder on the screen after some time. This used to make the touch screen stop working effectively after some time. Though smartphones like Palm were available in the late 1990s, customers at that time still did not have a mindset to utilize the many features of a smartphone. It was only after mid 2000s, that a large number of customers became aware of the utility of these features and started asking for these features. Further, with intense competition in the telecom industry, the prices for data plans were reduced by telecom companies. These data plans became affordable for the masses and demand for smartphones increased. After Apple's iPhone became popular, many competing products were launched using Android technology, some as early as in an year's time, but iPhone was able to create its brand image during this period. Apple's iPhone had a multi-touch screen which was the first in smart phones. Android based phones like HTC also launched a number of products like HTC Aria later with their own multi-touch screen phones. Many cellular phones now are being launched with a 2-camera feature, one camera for taking pictures and another one for doing video conferencing, to utilize the 4G network. However, there are many customers who are able to utilize this video conference feature owing to bandwidth limitations and the fact that the person they are calling may not have a similar phone. Therefore, some products are launched ahead of their time and companies need to assess if the customers are ready to adapt to new technologies and utilize their features.

Software Services Industry: Copying the IBM Model?

Within the same Industry, different players adopt slightly different approaches to solving the customer's needs. Some of these players specialize in one particular need of the customer while other ones try to position themselves as a one stop shop for all the customer needs. In the case of IT services business, there are many players like IBM, Accenture, Deloitte, Cognizant and India based companies like TCS, Wipro, Infosys etc. Each of these have taken different approaches to solving the needs of customers. Companies like Accenture and Deloitte started as consulting services for Accounts Auditing, Finance and risk management and still thrive in those domains. Their software services grew as they had access to the Chief Finance Officers and Chief Information Officers of various organizations. These companies did not have expertise in IT Infrastructure services like IBM, but had strength in business domain areas. These companies have maintained their brand images as specializing in the accounts auditing, management consulting, financial advisory and risk management activities and do not prefer to be primarily known as software services companies. IBM was primarily a IT hardware manufacturing company and IT Infrastructure services organization till the 1980s. In the 1990s, CEO Lou Gerstner repositioned IBM to move towards becoming a services organization. IBM also did many acquisitions to grow its software products division. The key selling point of IBM was to be a one-stop shop to large corporations to provide Hardware, Software and Services. It would offer to maintain the hardware and software and would also offer to write application software to serve the needs of the customer.

To grow its software products division, IBM started acquiring many software product companies in the 1990s. It acquired Lotus Notes for utilizing workflow based applications using email backbone in organizations. IBM expanded into a new class of software the Middleware software: between the front end/GUI software for customer interaction and the backend software that is the Database Layer or the Mainframe based layer. IBM created a new Websphere brand composed of middleware software products. One of the first products in this group was an Application Server which was a middle tier between the web based front end and the back end database. Later, it added many other products like MQ (message queue) which ensured asynchronous delivery of messages between multiple software components; and a Message Broker system working as a hub in a hub and spoke architecture where the central hub manages work and message flows between different groups in an organization, many times using distinctly different technologies. Similarly, to strengthen its presence in the data analytics domain, IBM purchased Cognos which was a strong player in user driven reports and also purchased Datastage which had a strong ETL (Extraction Transformation and Loading) tool to be used for creation of large data warehouses. IBM focused software products available on Unix and Windows operating systems rather than just being available on mainframes, as Unix and Windows became popular in the Industry in the 1990s.

IBM is preferred by Chief technology officers of many large organizations as in case of any hardware or software glitch, the CTO can direct the single point person of IBM to get the problem resolved using the resources of IBM. The Chief technology officer does not need to coordinate with different vendors and specially does not have to deal with the passing of buck by various vendors. IBM's success in providing a complete end-to-end sales and services of all IT components has been an envy of other large IT companies. Hewlett Packard also has been trying to position itself on the lines of IBM. HP was a strong player in IT Hardware business but did not have a strong presence in software products or software services. HP has tried to grow its services division by acquisitions. A services company Mphasis, based out of Bangalore, India with over 30,000 employees was acquired by Hewlett Packard to grow its services division. Oracle Corporation, which started as a Database company but grew into a software company by growing middleware and ERP products acquired Sun Microsystems to become a solution provider offering both hardware and software. However, the services division of Oracle is still very small and caters mainly to service its products. During late 1990s and early 2000s, IBM realized that despite being the only end-to-end solution provider, it cannot compete with companies from India due to the cost advantage of these companies as they were developing application software from a lower cost center based in India. Sometime around mid 2000s, Infosys chairman Mr N. R. Narayan Murthy declared that American companies cannot compete with Indian companies as Indian companies have mastered the art of 'Global delivery'. Perhaps, he revealed about his corporate strength more openly than what he should have.

From around 2005, IBM started growing its India based center and reducing its American services division to copy this 'Global delivery' model. IBM is now the largest private sector employer in India. Though IBM and HP have moved aggressively into services division, they have not been able to stop the growth of Indian services companies. IBM and HP's work culture is still inherited from a hardware vendor selling in a seller's market. IBM inherits the deep "techy" culture where except Lou Gerstner, none of the IBM CEOs in the last 30 years has had a management degree. IBM delivery managers had their reach with the Chief Technology Officers of client organizations, whereas Deloitte and Accenture, owing to having a heritage of Auditing and financial consulting backgrounds, had relations with Chief Executive Officers and Chief Information Officers. In order to overcome this weakness, in 2002, IBM had acquired Price Waterhouse Coopers's consulting group and tried to move towards a partner based model. IBM has believed in the concept of "work-life balance" for its employees. This culture is different from what I call a "work-work balance" of wall street companies where many employees have to work till midnight every day. Indian companies are able to survive and thrive in this 24 hour work culture as they have global teams and a work culture to support this type of non-stop development work. IBM, despite having the same cost advantage that Indian companies have, is not able to displace the Indian companies. As application software development and maintenance is the core strength and bread and butter of Indian companies, Indian companies understand the business domain and nuances of individual clients.

As IBM has more employees outside United States than inside United States and it is now being considered even a lower paying company to its employees than many India based companies, IBM needs to re-assess what has been the impact on its brand image.

Pricing:

Another issue which IT companies face is how to get paid for different types of services. While all IT services work is charged on hourly basis, companies have yet to distinguish themselves in terms of the quality of work. The price of a long term software development project and the price of a three day troubleshooting of Infrastructure issue are both being determined based on the number of hours to be spent on the project. However, the nature of these two tasks is very different. While it makes sense to use the number of hours for pricing a long term software development work, the work of troubleshooting an immediate technical problem is of a different nature. If a consultant for the latter project is aware that the price for his work would be based on the number of hours he spends troubleshooting, he would have incentive to take longer to fix the issue, instead of doing it faster. In this case, a consultant with better skills who is able to determine the problem and solve it faster would bill less number of hours and would get less paid compared to a consultant who has poor skills and takes much longer to troubleshoot the issues.

Another strong leader has emerged in the last decade in this Industry, New Jersey based Cognizant. Cognizant has combined the advantage of having an American client facing team and a cost-effective India based delivery team. While India based companies have delivery mangers promoted from within the software development teams and generally have little US based education, most delivery managers in Cognizant are Americans and alumni of leading US business schools and universities. Cognizant focuses mainly on the application software development and maintenance activities and boasts strong domain expertise in many Industries. The three pronged approach of Domain expertise, Global delivery and American client facing managers gives Cognizant a strong expertise over other players.

As we discussed earlier in this chapter, Corporate strategy is a process innovation of alternate means where these various means are employed for the end result of higher profitability. Companies outsourcing their business processes to outside consulting organizations are doing this process innovation to save costs. But this is for short term profitability. Once domain knowledge of in-house business processes is shared with outside consulting/ software service organizations, the secrets of business processes are also revealed to the these consulting organizations. Over a period of time, these secrets would get shared with other competitors and would impact the long term profitability of corporations outsourcing their services. Therefore, organizations need to assess which software solutions should be outsourced to outside organizations and which of these should be maintained in-house.

It may be noticed from this discussion that each of these players in this industry started with strengths in certain areas but lagged in other areas. While each tried to overcome the weaker areas by adding new capabilities, they needed others in the Industry to provide a complete solution to satisfy the client requirements. As was discussed earlier in this chapter, this Industry utilized addition methodology to increase its capability using internal resources as well as resources from other organizations. It applied the strategy of 'co-opitition' or cooperating with other players to grow their businesses together.

Creating Brand Value on Internet:

While innovating and bringing new products, a corporation needs to consider the impact on its brand image from its every single move. Amazon.com started as a mere book seller on internet, but kept enhancing its image due to continuous improvement to user and continuous enhancement of the services and products being offered to the customer. Further, a user's experience on Amazon.com has been increasingly friendly despite the vastly more number of products and services. Customers could purchase a $199 'Kindle Fire' on Amazon.com in its pre-sales orders without looking or feeling it, as the customers have full faith on Amazon.com's ability to understand their needs. Customers are aware that Amazon.com would ensure that it would take care of the customer. If Amazon.com is not able to deliver a purchased product, it credits the customer without the customer asking for the credit.

(the picture above is that of Kindle Fire, a tablet launched by Amazon, which is different from the e-ink based reading device kindle. Kindle Fire is competing with Apple's iPAD)

Providing such a user experience has been difficult to many other internet based services. A major internet based auction website for example charges nearly $200 from individual users to just list the Car. Many customers are not able to sell their Cars on the website, despite paying this fee. It would be safe to assume that the user experience of these customers is at the best unpleasant. What is the probability that the user would return back to use the website after losing $200 in his first experience. Perhaps, the company needs to create a process where part of the amount charged in an unsuccessful selling effort is credited towards some purchase or selling another article on this website. This would ensure that customer keeps coming back to the website and give a positive user experience to the user. Many customers prefer ethnic focused clones of major web site. For example, people from South Asia prefer to utilize Sulekha. com's classifieds advertisements for buying and selling their things due to higher comfort level owing to language and culture. An example of the original innovation is Hotmail.com, an internet based email portal. However, a similar internet based email service was later launched by Yahoo.com. Yahoo.com quickly became popular owing to it being launched by the most popular web portal in late 1990s. Additionally, Yahoo.com introduced a powerful junk mail removing algorithm in its engine which made it popular. Later, Google introduced Gmail which also become very popular, but Google also runs analysis on the emails of users to profile the users. Google uses the information to display advertisements of interest to the email users, but many users feel this is invasion of their privacy. Perhaps, there is a growing demand for paid email service where users can be sure of their privacy concerns.

Many times there are cultural differences which can be utilized to create regional clone websites of major portals. Rediff.com and Rediffmail are successful India based internet portal and mail service sites, which became popular in the 1990s. Rediff became popular in India owing to its understanding of the cultural differences and having a first mover advantage in that country.

Major portals like Yahoo and hotmail did not focus their attention outside the western world in the 1990s.

These examples tell us that internet based companies can utilize addition and combination methodologies to increase the number of features and their utility for customers. Many internet based companies also use transposition to create local versions of other popular websites.

INNOVATION AND MERGERS AND ACQUISITIONS:

With intense pressure from wall street analysts to show growth every quarter, CEOs are constantly striving to keep the stock prices high to satisfy the shareholders. Further, a large part of executive pay is based on stock options and is therefore linked to the stock price. If the stock price goes down, the value of these options is minuscule or nil.

A company with high cash has mainly two choices: either distribute the cash as dividend or utilize it to grow the organization. Distributing dividends gives a signal to wall street that managers are running short of ideas in growing the organization and it reduces the stock price. Thus, managers are left with the second choice, that of utilizing this cash to somehow grow the business.

Utilizing this cash to grow the organization organically requires long gestation period, creativity and marketing efforts. So, an easier way for the managers is to spend this cash to buy another company. Thus, excess cash in public companies is utilized to acquire other companies. Cash worth many Billions is spent by large companies every year in the name of mergers and acquisitions.

Top management requires little efforts to acquire another company besides utilizing the efforts of investment bankers.

It takes around an year to complete an acquisition process and a few more years to complete the amalgamation of the two companies. Acquiring organizations usually have to overpay, sometimes substantially, to purchase the shares from shareholders of the target company to be acquired. The reason provided for this overpaying has been that the "synergy" created with the merger would grow the organization rapidly. However, It can take many years to find out if there was any benefit to the organization due to "synergy" from the acquisition.

The premium paid above the book value to purchase the new organization would depreciate shareholders' value, unless the "synergy" comes into play.

While some acquisitions have given increased revenues and earnings to the combined organizations, many shareholders have now started questioning the rationale behind these acquisitions and have started asking whether these acquisitions have been adding value to the organizations.

To explore whether M&A adds or reduces value for shareholders, let us consider a few examples of M&A:

- Intel and Microsoft have been blamed and even sued for not allowing competition due to their size and market dominance. These companies being the leaders of their Industry have huge Research and Development budgets, marketing budgets and cash to purchase smaller competing companies. These companies have also created standards for Computer Chips and Operating Systems on personal computers and are able to create barriers which make it difficult for other companies to enter these businesses. However, the prices of their products have been falling and an average personal computer costs less than one third of what it used to cost 20 years ago, so it is debatable if the acquisitions these companies have done has been able to kill competition and keep the prices high.

- The price of gasoline in US retail gas stations has never come down below $1 per gallon after the merger of Exxon and Mobil in late 1990s. Consumers also get suspicious when they are cited examples of a price increase after a major merger. Many times the government does not allow mergers and acquisition by major companies suspecting that these mergers would lead to monopolies and price increases for average consumers.

- Coca Cola and Pepsi have been purchasing other food and drink companies as they can make additional sales through existing supply chain. Consumer product companies have expansion capacity in their supply chain and can utilize this capacity to sell additional number of products. These companies make acquisitions of companies with new products so that they can utilize their economies of scale in selling additional products with existing resources.

- Many companies try to utilize their brand images and management skills to grow the acquired businesses. Starbucks Coffee purchased Jamba Juice maker Evolution Fresh in 2011 for $30 million. The Evolution Fresh company uses a high pressurizing technique of keeping the juice fresh for long period. Starbucks has made the acquisition so that it can utilize its brand image and marketing strength to grow the Jamba Juice business.

- One of the famous cases where the "merger" was a failure and caused shareholder value destruction was the merger of Germany's major automaker Daimler AG with Chrysler. Daimler's investment to merge with Chrysler in 1998 was calculated to be $37 Billion. In 2007, nearly nine years later after the acquisition and in-spite of making all efforts, when Daimler's leadership could not get the "Synergy", it sold 80% of Chrysler to Cerberus Capital, a private equity firm in United States for $7 Billion using a demerger process. To "sell" the remaining 20% of Chrysler, Daimler had to "pay" 650 million dollars to contribute towards the pension fund of former employees of Chrysler. Later, even Cerberus Capital was not successful in turning around the company and in 2009, Chrysler filed for bankruptcy protection.

Innovation for adding value to M&A transactions:

After studying many such mergers and acquisitions, it is apparent to me that overpaying during acquisitions is justified only when an acquisition can give a company some pricing power. If the pricing power is not attained, simply joining the two companies for adding revenues and earnings does not add value to the shareholders. That would be equivalent to taking the cash which belonged to the shareholder and giving him one combined stock , instead of two stocks from different firms. The shareholder could have purchased the stocks of the acquired company on his own with the cash that belonged to him, even without the two companies joining together.

Organizations should be concerned about increasing profitability and shareholder value and not just growing top line (sales). A growth in the top line (revenues)without a simultaneous higher growth in the bottom line (profits) does not add any value to the shareholders.

While economies of scale is a good argument, either of the companies could have grown bigger to get that economy of scale on its own. Pricing power would add to the profits of the company which increases shareholder value. Pricing power could be attained by many ways: It could be owing to market share dominance as in the case of Exxon and Mobil merger. Or it could be by creating higher barriers to entry in that industry. It could also be based on utilizing government regulations available to the acquired company that protects a market segment. For example, acquiring a company which has exclusive rights to sell a product in a particular geography gives pricing power to a purchasing company.

If none of these are applicable, it needs to be questioned if it will lead to innovation by joining together the products or skills of the two companies. If the cost of getting these products or skills from the market is lower than the cost of acquiring the new entity, there will be little addition to the shareholders value from this M&A transaction. But if the acquired company has unique and specialized technology and skills which can be utilized by the products of the acquiring company, it can lead to enhancing the pricing power of the acquiring company. One example is the acquisition of Sequent Corporation in 2000 by IBM. IBM utilized the patented technology of Sequent with which Sequent could run multiple versions of the operating system on the same computer and even able to run multiple operating systems (like Windows and Unix) on the same computer hardware. IBM utilized this technology in its other products, after the acquisition.

INNOVATION and MARKETING:

Let us explore if we can utilize innovation as a tool for marketing. Many frameworks have been proposed by Management Experts for marketing strategy. Some have focused on targeting existing set of customers, where as others have recommended identifying and targeting new customer segments. In 2005, W Chan Kim and Renee Mauborgne from INSEAD published the concept of Blue Ocean Strategy for corporations. They have proposed that in order to be successful, a company should do 'value innovation' or add value with innovation while simultaneously reducing unneeded functions and parts to reduce the cost. This way the company adds value of the product or service for both itself as well as the customers. They have proposed using the value innovation to find new set of customers.

Blue ocean strategy relies on innovation to create or alter products and service, recommends reducing unnecessary features and target a new set of customers.

Here are a few examples and thoughts on applying innovation techniques for strategy and marketing by some organizations:

Sintex, A success story from 1980s:

In many emerging countries, water supply is rationed; water is supplied to homes and offices for only a few hours during the day. People store water for the remaining hours, using a rooftop water tank. This water tank used to be made from Cement till the 1970s. The Cement Tank had many issues: It was too heavy to be carried up the building and had to be constructed on the site, which used to take many days. Sometimes, the cement tank would leak after a few years and would develop Algae. An alternate solution was provided by Ahmedabad, India based Sintex Corporation. It created a plastic tank which was light, strong and could be easily carried to rooftops. It would not corrode, get cracks or leak for a very long time. This simple innovative product became a hot selling product in many emerging countries in Asia and Africa. Sintex Industries is now the largest water tank selling company in the world. The simplicity of installation as well as the durability of the product has given a strong brand image to the company and the company. The company has now developed other durable and strong plastic based products that are light in weight and easy to move and install. Sintex has developed pre-fabricated housing and green technologies among many innovative products. The company has used alternate means methodology of innovation as a strategy to find new markets and grow in those markets. It has utilized its strength in manufacturing of plastic products.

Tall Mast of McDonald's:

A large number of fast food customers are drivers, who stop on the highways. As the traffic on highways is very fast, if the driver does not observe a restaurant at least half a mile away, he would not be able to make up his mind, slow down and exit from the highway towards the restaurant. Some successful fast food restaurants like McDonald's have realized this problem and put up very tall masts in front of the restaurants. Customers driving their cars can see from almost half a mile away that they are approaching a McDonald's restaurant and have nearly a minute to make up their mind and exit from the highway or street to the restaurant.

Oversize It, To Hang Out:

I observed are two restaurants in Ahmedabad, one selling egg based dining products and another one selling Indian food targeting the truck drivers. It is hard to ignore these businesses even though they are located on crowded streets. The first one has a supersized model of an egg, almost 12 feet large attached to its outer wall. The second one has the shell of the front part of the truck attached outside, it looks like a truck is coming out of the wall of this restaurant.

Attached below is another example: the picture of a supersized model of a Duracell battery in a supermarket in US, used to draw attention of passing customers. Compare the size of this model to the actual batteries.

COCA COLA's image problems:

For the last few years, a lot has been said against coca cola and the bad health effects from it, specially attributing childhood obesity to it. Due to this, a decline has been observed in the sales growth of the main cola product. The company has diversified into other products like water, lemon-based products, fruit-drinks and non-soda based products.

Coca Cola advertisements use big celebrities but the masses are still worried about the harmful effects of sugar based drinks.

It is surprising to me that not a single advertisement has been aired about the fact that coca cola was created as a health drink by a doctor to cure patients and give them a positive feeling.

In fact many people drink coca cola on a daily basis to get relief from the symptoms of acidity and indigestion. Perhaps, Coke could utilize this aspect of the drink to create a positive awareness about the drink.

Value Addition By Pre-Cutting The Vegetables:

It is always surprising to see that there is no end to innovation in the simplest of products, services and processes. Recently, I came across some vegetable sellers in India where they had pre-cut vegetables and were selling these at a higher price than regular vegetables to customers.

People selling these vegetables are mostly illiterate or barely educated. However, they could realize that consumers these days are always short of time and would be willing to pay a little extra if they can save their time by buying pre-cut vegetables.

In USA, this is being done for a long time for certain vegetables like peas or carrots. Here, the pre-cut and sometimes semi-prepared vegetables are sold in sealed plastic bags. These bags are kept refrigerated in retail stores. This value addition helps in fetching a higher price.

Tata Creating Super Cheap Homes:

After creating world's cheapest car Nano, India's Tata Group is trying to use the same concept to create cheapest homes. This house expected to cost around six hundred US dollars will be made up of pre-fabricated material which can be assembled onsite in a few days period. The size of the rooms will be small and the house will be only 20 sq meters. However, with hundreds of millions of people across the globe, a strong roof and walls to cover them would be a boon. The product has been designed by using an assembly line manufacturing concept to the house construction. Further the use of pre-fabricated material which is light but strong has also added to this design. The innovation methodology of transposition and alternate means are being utilized for this product.

(The above picture is of a fabricated structure being sold in a superstore in US)

Internet on TV versus TV on Internet:

When the internet first started becoming popular in the early 1990s, many homes did not have Personal computers. Laptop computers were very expensive and only a few companies used to provide these to their employees. Many hotels in America started providing Internet services on the set top box of a TV set. Users had basic functionality of typing a web site name, scrolling on the screen and clicking, with a wireless keyboard.

However, as Personal computers and Laptop computers became increasingly affordable, the need to browse on a TV set was not required. As almost all the companies started providing laptop computers to employees, many Hotels started providing Wi-Fi based internet connectivity.

Further, the speed of the internet connectivity became fast and it enabled watching video on internet. Youtube.com became popular due to this ability of internet to carry large amounts of video based data to people's homes.

This has now resulted in many content providing TV channels being available via internet which people can watch on their personal computers.

Many modern gaming systems like Nintendo's Wii has blurred the difference between TV and Internet as they provide the capability to browse internet on TV as well as provide the functionality of group online gaming on TV with other users, utilizing the internet connection available on TV's Cable.

SATELLITE DISH TV through CABLE (actually internet cable) !

The concept of receiving TV content through a Satellite signal, also called Dish TV started becoming popular in the 1990s. It was giving competition to the cable based TV companies and was usable in remote areas where Cable TV networks were not available. Many of these DISH TV channels were international TV Channels.

More than 20 years after it started, DISH TV has started utilizing high speed internet for selling its content to viewers. Dish TV is offering an IPTV box which once connected to high speed internet at a user's home or office, would be able to receive TV channels signals. This obviates the need to install a Satellite signal receiver (called DISH).

Now a large percentage of homes in the US get their internet connection through their cable TV company. Many users have the option to switch off their TV services and just utilize the internet line for their Internet based TV.

The Dish TV company realized that users are purchasing it's services because of content and do not care about the medium. The users would be willing to pay for the content whether it is coming from Satellite based receiver, Cable network or an Internet connection.

The company cares about the revenues and decided to utilize additional transmission medium. The company has utilized alternate means methodology for marketing its product to new customers.

It is interesting that the company is utilizing a medium it was supposed to give competition to.

The long time company took to utilize this new medium highlights the lag required in various stages of innovation.

Chipotle VS Taco bell:

TACO Bell is a popular Mexican Fast Food Chain in USA owned by Pepsico since 1978. It has aggressively grown to more than 6500 branches, selling Mexican food like Burritos and Tacos. The price of food items is very less, sometimes less than $3.00 but the quantity is also small as it targets a large number of children as its customers. Many American customers prefer to take their children to Taco Bell instead of McDonald's due to the perceived health benefits of Mexican food. Overall, Taco Bell targets families with small children as its primary customers. Taco Bell uses the picture of a Bell as its logo that is perceived to be attractive to children.

Chipotle, another Mexican restaurant targets Adults. It offers the same mexican food like Burritos and Tacos, but in bigger sizes, usually one item is large enough for a single meal of a person. These usually cost above $7.00, but since the size is enough for a single meal, many customers prefer it. To give it a complete adult experience, the restaurant also offers Alcoholic Beer.

While the food is the same Mexican food, these two chains have identified a different set of customers and have utilized slightly different variations of food and ambience.

9

PERILS OF THE VENTURE CAPITAL INDUSTRY:

. . . .

*"*The probability of an entrepreneur getting venture capital is the same as getting struck by lightning while standing at the bottom of a swimming pool on a sunny day. This may be too optimistic." Guy Kawasaki (founding partner of Garage Technology Ventures and author of The Art of the Start)*

United States may be called the land of innovation and venture capital industry in the 20th century. In the beginning, it was private individuals who used to provide risk capital to early stage companies. For example, It was J P Morgan who supported and financed Mr Thomas Edison to start new ventures based on the electricity based patents of Mr Edison.

Later, the US government realizing that development of new products and services would be essential to grow the country's economy, made policies to support early stage companies. Knowing that it was difficult for these early stage companies to get bank loans as these companies had limited or no assets which could be used as collateral, government created laws to encourage Pension Funds, Endowment funds and other financial organizations to invest part of their funds in risky early stage companies. As the name Venture essentially meant risk, capital being invested into these early stage companies was called venture capital. From 1950s, these policies greatly supported the venture capital industry in United States.

Easier availability of risk capital and strong infrastructure drew entrepreneurs from around the world to United States. As an example, Vinod Khosla, founder of Sun Microsystems, tried to start a small soy milk company in New Delhi, India before coming to United States. However, he was not successful due to a difficult environment for entrepreneurs in India those days and decided to move to the silicon valley.

The concept of Venture capital as an industry grew after 1950s. Professional money managers, who were generally highly qualified individuals and had some financial industry experience, would get funds from financial entities like Pension funds and Endowment funds. These individuals would start a Limited Partnership firm where they would invest in promising early stage ventures in the form of equity, debt or convertible-debt. (a form of debt that is convertible to equity at a later time). These Venture funds would invest in the early stage companies, monitor their accounts and also help in business development activities. After a few years of growing these firms, the venture funds would sell their stake in these companies. Many times the sale price of these investments would fetch them high returns. The purchaser of these stakes would be either large corporations, the entrepreneurs themselves or through the stock market, if the company went public. Though some venture investments would fail, still the returns from successful ventures would make up for the losses from bad investments and give overall good returns. The venture capital industry in United States has helped the development and growth of many major corporations. Many famous technology companies got their initial investments from venture capital firms.

However, the Venture Capital Industry has witnessed some fundamental challenges during the last decade. During the first decade of 2000s, pure Venture Capital Industry has given negative real returns to investors. Venture Capital Industry has faced a talent crunch both in finding good investment managers as well as in finding good entrepreneurs.

Challenge of finding good fund managers:

As the Venture Capital Industry grew, the number of professional money managers (called FUND Managers) also grew. The qualification to become a Fund manager was the ability to raise capital from financial institutions like Pension Funds and Endowment Funds or high net worth individuals. Some former entrepreneurs became VCs due to their proximity with the Venture Capital Industry. Some of these were successful in their prior ventures, but some were unsuccessful in their ventures. Many times, it was people working in finance industry, primarily the investment bankers, who had the network to raise the capital. Not necessarily, all of these individuals had the skills to identify upcoming technologies, identify good entrepreneurs or do business development for portfolio companies. Sometimes, the venture capital industry would hire retired senior government officials as they had the reputation and influence to help raise capital from public entities. Former Vice President Al Gore had joined Kleiner Perkins, one of the largest Venture Capital firms. David Rubenstein, a former aide to President Jimmy Carter in the White House started Carlyle, one of the largest venture capital and LBO (Leveraged Buyout) firms. Other times, former CEOs of large corporations also joined Venture capital companies as they had the reputation to raise capital as well as had the management skills and business development skills. Lou Gerstner, former CEO of IBM Corporation joined The Carlyle group after retiring from IBM. While some of these executives have been very successful in identifying good early stage companies and growing early stage companies, many have not been successful. The reputation and industry contacts have been helpful to these professionals in raising capital, but many of them lacked the skills and experience to identify new technologies, identify good entrepreneurs and grow early stage companies.

What attracts people to this Industry:

One of the reasons why many people with widely ranging backgrounds have been attracted to the "VC Industry", has been the remuneration structure.

Traditionally, the General Partners, or those people who raise funds from Limited Partners (usually organizations like Pension Funds, Endowment Funds, large Finance Organizations), charge a fixed management fee every year. Usually, this fee is 2% of the value of the size of the fund. Additionally, they get "carry" or Carried over interest, which is a % of the profits above a threshold limit. This fees is generally 20% of the profits returned back to the limited partners, above a threshold limit. This threshold limit usually has been around 12%.

So, here is the Math:

John and Mike, two former investment bankers decide to raise their own Venture Capital Fund. They raise a $100 million from a Pension Fund. The Fund is to be returned in 7 years time. The fee agreement is traditional, i.e. 2% of the fund size every year and a carry of 20% of the profits above an IRR of 12%.

With a traditional fee agreement, they collect $2 million (2% of the fund) every year for 7 years, which comes to a total of $14 million. They are ensured of this fee even if the fund does not give any returns to the investor and even if the fund ends up losing money on investments.

In case they are able to make good investments, grow the portfolio companies and exit with high profitability, they make further money as carried interest.

As an example, if they return the money after 7 years at an IRR of 20%, they make an additional $27 million in carried interest (Returns at 20% IRR = 358 million, Returns at 12% IRR = 221 million, Difference is $137 million. 20% of $137 million is paid as carried interest which comes to $27 million).

However, they could also raise another bigger fund, which would result in guaranteed fees. So, If they raise their next fund of $250 million, they make just the management fees of $5 million per year for 7 years, which comes to $35 million.

So, instead of focusing on their current fund, almost immediately after raising the first fund (called closing the fund in Venture Capital Industry parlance), they start raising the next fund, usually of a much bigger size.

While the newer Venture Capital Industry agreements have tightened management fee structures, for example the 2% management fees is paid only on the amount actually in investment mode, still this management fees many times comes to be larger than the "carry", when the investments do not give the expected returns.

CURE:

To cure the Venture Capital Industry from this issue, where many General Partners are focused mostly on fund raising, while giving secondary importance to investment and business development work, the fee structure needs to change. The management fees should not constantly increase based on the size of the fund, but should have an upper limit, based on the remuneration requirements of the general partners, staff and other administrative expenses. There could be an element of bonus based on investments and exits made every year, but almost all the returns to the General partners should be based on the final returns on the fund given back to the limited partners. This would attract resources to the fund who have real talent and desire in finding good opportunities of making investments and doing business development. This fee structure would force the fund managers to give primary importance to giving returns to the investors rather than raising larger funds.

Finding a Good Entrepreneur and Company:

The second challenge which the Venture Capital Industry faces is how to identify good entrepreneurs, especially in early stage companies. In my experience working with entrepreneurs of early stage companies, I found that many entrepreneurs are less professional and less hard working than many employees of their companies.

Most of these companies are very small and are barely breaking even. It is hard to predict which of these managers would be able to grow the companies. Venture Capitalists have to meet and deal with many types of entrepreneurs. Some entrepreneurs have high energy levels but may be not be having the wisdom and patience, others are too content with just a little growth and do not have the vision to grow the firm.

There are some entrepreneurs who start companies for the purpose of attaining a social status. For them, the goal of growing the company and selling it later for profits, is not important. Owning a company, however small it may be and being a boss is the cherished goal of many people. Some such entrepreneurs, once they get venture capital funding lose all interest in growing the company. Instead of focusing on business development, they spend their time socializing, networking and public speaking in various forums. Sometimes, they could justify these actions saying that these activities help in marketing the company's products and making people aware of the company, though the target customers may not even be attending such forums. Such behavior from an entrepreneur is fine as long as the capital employed in the formation of the company is not from an outside investor. If a venture capitalist has invested money in a company started by such an entrepreneur, the Venture Capitalist would like the entrepreneur to focus all his energies towards growing the company and provide an early exit route to the Venture Capitalist, so that the Venture Capitalist gets timely returns on his capital. One Venture Capitalist once told me that If the entrepreneur's company is growing very slowly and even after many years, is not attaining the size required to give the Venture capital firm a good exit, the company is nothing but a "lifestyle" company. Such a "lifestyle" company just exists to support the lifestyle of the CEO/ entrepreneur. The investor is not able to get any returns on his investment into this firm.

There have been cases of many entrepreneurs who have tried to siphon off funds from the company to recover their personal investment in the company. There are some young entrepreneurs who get egoistic and do not have the discipline to follow regulations and patience to grow the company for a long period. Most Venture Capitalists appoint their own accountants/auditors in the portfolio company to get feedback about the status of the company and identify any unethical accounting practices.

VCs sometimes also have to deal with the "techy" entrepreneurs. These entrepreneurs though are very good in technology, but are not able to sell their products as they do not have marketing skills and are not able to explain the business use of their products. One of such entrepreneurs I met took two hours to explain what his product does. After listening to him for two hours, I realized that he has developed a product to enable making payment using mobile phones. I realized the reason he was not able to sell his product for more than five years was because he just could not explain his concepts in business terms. Once a proper sales pitch was prepared for him, he was able to get a big client in a few months time. Many times the techy entrepreneurs prefer to hire other techies for sales jobs. They would benefit with hiring pure sales people, may be with the support the Venture Capital firm.

Some entrepreneurs are focused on building the product but lose focus of other important aspects of business like pricing power. Their companies find themselves in a situation where all the pricing power is in the hands of the buyer. Companies with non-unique products or having only a few large customers find themselves in such a situation. If the company is a captive supplier to a giant customer like Walmart, the pricing power is controlled by the customer. Similarly, for many Mobile Value Added Services companies (which provide cellular phone based services like finding train schedule, booking a ticket etc), giant telecom companies are the direct customers, and they control the pricing.

Successful entrepreneurs are good at both technology and sales, and are willing to listen and learn from VCs and senior executives to grow their businesses.

Many entrepreneurs are just not able to maintain the accounts, comply with regulations and do the general management tasks. These individuals need repeated instructions from the Venture Capitalist and support from the auditors. It is best for such entrepreneurs to stick to the product development area and allow some other professional to take the lead in general management tasks.

Very successful entrepreneurs like Jeff Bezos and Steve Jobs are not stuck with just one product idea, but constantly use innovation to keep adding the list of products and features.

Using Venture Capital funds for Private Equity investments:

There is no measurement system available to identify good fund managers for the venture capital industry. This makes it difficult for the Venture Capital Industry to find good fund managers. Shortage of good fund managers who could identify good investment opportunities and grow companies has changed the basic nature of the industry over the last two decades. As many money managers have purely finance backgrounds and may not have the skills or experience to evaluate new technologies or judge the potential of a new entrepreneur, they develop fear of investing money in early stage companies. The fear of losing money on investments in early stage companies has made many of these Venture Capital fund managers to look for "non-ventures" while making "venture" investments. These fund managers look for companies which are profitable and are in operation for many years. Investing in these type of established companies cannot be defined as a risky investment or "venture". These established companies many times are even capable of taking bank debt but prefer to raise money by privately issuing shares to these "venture capital" companies. Therefore, since many of these Venture Capital firms are providing private capital in the form of equity to companies, these are also called Private Equity companies.

Some Venture Capital fund managers with investment banking backgrounds have also created an LBO (leveraged buy out) model. Instead of investing in early stage companies, an LBO firm buys all the equity of a public company from the stock market. After making this company private, these firms re-engineer the balance sheet to have much higher level of debt. Many times, the LBO firm has an arrangement with banks for debt for the company while using the assets of the company as collateral. In 1988, the Leveraged buy out firm KKR & Co purchased RJR Nabisco for $25 Billion, still considered to be the largest Leveraged buyout of history. Henry Kravis, the founder of KKR is now also known as the father of the LBO business.

Many times, the general partners of the private equity firms focus on satisfying the limited partners' concerns and raising fresh capital. The business development task is given to consultants or former employees of top rated Consultancy firms like McKinsey and Bain. However, these consultants may not have experience of working in and growing a start up company as their consulting experience is mostly with large MNCs. Only large MNCs can afford their hourly consultancy charges (as high as $1000 per hour in many cases).

To grow an early stage company requires both patience and compassion for the entrepreneur. In the past, there have been some famous cases where the VCs harshly treated the entrepreneurs and unceremoniously removed them. Some in the media also coined the word "Vulture Capitalists" for such Venture Capitalists in the 1990s, who forced the founding CEO of the company to leave his own company. Steve Jobs was an example of one such CEO: Steve jobs founded Apple but was removed from Apple by the professional managers and board in 1985. He had to be brought back in by the board after the company started failing. Similarly, Sandy Lerner, the founder of CISCO, one of the largest IT companies in the world, was fired from the company in 1990, shortly after the company had gone public.

As these Venture Capital firms are almost always interested to invest at a growth stage where the company has crossed a few million dollars in revenues, many entrepreneurs have lamented that true early stage venture capital money has vanished and the so called "VC firms" are actually just Private Equity finance companies. Guy Kawasaki's comments quoted in the beginning of this chapter somewhat point to this fact.

PE or VC: What's in the name?:

Before working at a venture capital company, I tried for years to figure out how to quickly determine if something is a venture capital investment or a private equity investment. Some suggested that private equity is a super-umbrella term that is called venture capital when the investment is at an early stage. However, some companies have operated for 6-10 years before they come for venture funding.

Others conveyed that Venture capital is the original term which became popular after the 2nd world war and private equity is the term coined in the 80's after famous people like Henry Kravis invested in bigger companies.

Determining by size of the company also gets tricky, as revenue of $2 million might be considered small in a developed country but large in a developing country.

The size of the investment doesn't work either if you base it on country. An investment of $10 million in a US based company would be considered a venture investment, but might be considered a private equity investment in the developing world. Some professionals strictly define private equity as an LBO activity. But in developing countries like India, there is almost no LBO activity due to banking regulations, and yet billions of dollars are invested in large corporations by private equity players as equity or convertible debt. This sure looks like private equity investment, but does not fall under the LBO or MBO category.

There is also a conventional wisdom that says if a company is not yet successful but the promoter is very confident, it is a venture capital investment. Vice-versa, If a company is successful but the promoter is not that confident and wants to cash out or exit with restructuring or LBO, it is for sure a private equity investment. Though there may be some truth in that, it's not quite scientific enough and does not cover all investment scenarios.

So here's my own litmus test: if a company has no additional debt (bank-debt) carrying capacity due to its current financial state, an investment in it should be considered a venture capital investment. Otherwise, it should be considered a private equity investment. This should work for companies of all size, stage and in any country.

This article was written by the author and published on CBS public offering website in Apr 2008

Venture Capital Process:

In United States, the Venture Capital firms are formed with a legal structure called the limited partnership model. The Limited Partnership firm has a few General Partners who are responsible for making investments and giving returns to the Pension Funds, Endowment Funds and other investors who have invested their money with the Venture Capital firm. The investors in these venture capital firms are called as limited partners as their liability is limited to the investment they have made. In many Asian countries, a Venture Capital company is just another company and is called the management company. The fund is raised by a legal structure called a Trust. The Trust grants permission to the management company to manage the Venture Capital fund and pays the fund management fee as per agreement with the management company. In this structure, the fund manager has more freedom to leave the management company and leave the organization, especially if he finds a better opportunity or if his investments are not performing well. In a Limited Partnership firm, the general partners have an agreement with limited partners and they cannot leave till the term of the fund, which is usually from 7 to 10 years.

After a verbal understanding is reached between a Venture Capital firm and company seeking funds, the Venture Capital firm sends a term-sheet to the entrepreneur/owner of the company seeking funds. The term-sheet specifies the amount of money and the terms of investment offered by the Venture Capital firm. It also specifies the type of limitations the Venture Capital firm would put on the company to ensure that the company can be monitored by the Venture Capital firm. If the owners of the company agree to these terms, they accept the term-sheet. The term-sheet is generally not a binding agreement and is only an indicative offer of investment.

Sometimes, there are more negotiations after the term-sheet is signed. Once, the final terms are agreed upon, a legal Agreement is signed between the two sides, which is a binding agreement. Usually, the Venture Capital firm appoints its representative in the board of directors of this portfolio company, and puts restrictions on issuing of equity and debt by the company. The Venture Capital firm also appoints its own auditor in the portfolio company to get information on accounts. Other restrictions on hiring, changing board structure and remuneration structure are also put by the Venture Capital firm.

An escrow account is opened where the agreed amount of investment is kept in stages. Usually, representatives of both the Venture Capital firm and the portfolio company are joint signatories to withdraw money from this escrow account. The portfolio company issues stock or debt instruments either together or in stages to the Venture Capital firm, as per the agreement signed by them.

An alternative model:

After these formalities of investment process, monitoring of the portfolio company by the Venture Capital firm starts where the Venture Capital firm regularly meets the portfolio company's management team to monitor accounts and provide support for business development.

Due to the restrictions put on the entrepreneur, sometimes the entrepreneur has to spend considerable time satisfying the accounting and monitoring requirements of the Venture Capital firm. In many cases, the strategy, innovation and implementation of new ideas in the firm starts lagging as the startup company starts growing. Many times, the startup company relies on its founders for all skills and does not have funds to hire the best of marketing and product development staff.

An alternative model has been successfully implemented by IdeaLab, a company founded by Bill Gross. Here, the company generates its own product ideas using brainstorming of its core innovation team, who happen to be top professionals in their fields. Some of the core innovation team members are PhDs from top Universities and some have worked as Professors at Ivy League schools. It then hires and utilizes functional experts to create a prototype. Idealab uses its experienced marketing team to make tie-ups with external companies to produce and sell the products. Idealab is simultaneously working on many different products and is able to take the advantage of economies of scale. Idealab has produced some exceedingly innovative products and companies. Some of these products are mentioned in the previous chapter<>.

Value Investor versus the Power of Passion:

There are two distinct schools of thought in the business management education in United States. The first one encourages investing capital in risky-ventures and thus encourages startup ventures and venture capital Industry. Graduates from Stanford business school usually are known for starting up and leading major technology based companies.

The second school of thought encourages Value investing and encourages identifying companies which have stable financial track records, give regular dividends but are still available for a reasonable or 'value' price. Capital preservation is considered more important than growth opportunities for the sake of minimizing risk to the invested capital. Columbia business school is a leader in the Value investing principles. Mr Warren Buffet is the most famous alumnus of Columbia business school and has built enormous wealth identifying good stable but undervalued companies.

Value investors by nature avoid risk-taking and are looking for safe bets. Established business practices is what lures them. Value investors make investments in traditional companies with long track records of profitability. The investment is done at a price which is considered lower and below what the fundamental analysis of the company would suggest. Value investors may not be making as much money in years of intense volatility where the stock market has favored a particular Industry, but they are expected to make consistent and reasonable returns for a long time. Their investments also lose money during periods of recession but at a lower rate than the markets' favorites of previous years. To search for such companies, value investors look for companies with Low P/E (price to earnings ratio) ratios, consistent EPS (earnings per share) and regular and consistent high dividends. Value investors also prefer that the companies are leaders in their particular industries and that these industries have consistent high Earnings for a long time. Mr Warren Buffet defines this concept as "moats around the company" which means that the company must have something that gives it advantage over competition for a long time. Further, Mr Warren Buffet has stated that "When a good manager meets a bad Industry, the Industry usually wins". In other words, if you invest in an Industry which is going downhill, the chances of the company being profitable for a long time are low.

Unfortunately, Value investors fail to understand the power of Passion in business. If money was invested in Apple's stock in 2004, it would have grown fifty times by 2012. However, many famous value investors missed the opportunity and did not invest in Apple. Many entrepreneurs enter highly competitive or sometimes commodity businesses but still dramatically grow their companies due to their sheer passion for the business. When Amazon.com started selling books, it was written off by many value investors as they felt that just almost anybody can open a competing website selling books. As explained in an earlier chapter, Amazon.com created an eco-system of customer service thereby making it a default one stop choice for all internet based purchase. Amazon.com now sells a very large variety of products like electronics, shoes, garments and sports equipment. Amazon.com sells the products directly and also allows other vendors to sell through its website and compete with each other. Amazon.

com has also entered services business and is a strong force in the cloud computing space.Amazon.com has been able to give a personal touch to its customers where customers feel that they would be "taken care" of by Amazon. The comfort level of customers of Amazon.com is so good that it was able to pre-sell a large number of its Kindle Fire product, before it was launched in November 2011. Customers were ready to purchase a $199 product without ever touching or feeling it, and took the word of Amazon on face value.

Similarly, Apple Inc in 2000 was almost a bankrupt organization. But Steve Jobs grew it to be larger than Microsoft in only a decade. All the products which Steve jobs created like iPod, iPad, iPhone etc. were created with leading edge technologies which were available to other companies also. But, Steve Jobs with his passion was able to create new products at a faster pace and market them ahead of competition. An iPod was the first successful digital based music player which replaced the CD players of the 90s and Sony walkman of the 80s. Apple's iPhone was the first mobile phone product utilizing the technology of a multi-touch screen. Similarly, an iPad was the first successful touch screen digital pad. There were other companies which utilized similar technologies before Apple, but none could give an eco-system of marketing, technology and ergonomics to be successful.

The concept of Starbucks was only about selling coffee. It was a simple idea and there were tens of thousands of companies in United States which could have emulated his model and grown a chain of retail coffee stores. However, except 'seattle's Best Coffee', none of the other companies could grow like Starbucks. The Starbucks gives an ambiance of business environment and comfort. The ambiance of Starbucks includes an impressive interior-decoration, music, sofasets, WI-FI connections for internet, business newspapers and smart sales persons wearing impressive uniforms. This ambiance adds to the customer's feeling of luxury of choosing from a large variety of coffee drinks. The ambiance of Starbucks makes it ideal for many people to meet for short business meetings at an affordable price. The high price of Starbucks makes it appealing for people to carry the coffee cup as an icon of status symbol. In order to maximize its profits and give uniform experience in its stores, Starbucks does not give franchises but owns all its retail outlets and keeps the employees on payroll offering them long term career opportunities. Starbucks has created an eco system giving an optimum customer experience.

When Sam Walton was growing Walmart, he gave an offer to Mr Warren Buffet to invest in it. However, Mr Warren Buffet, being a value investor did not see any value in this retail business. He saw it as another retail store company and retail businesses were supposed to be low margin businesses with intense competition. Mr. Buffet could not appreciate the power of passion of Sam Walton. Sam Walton was a very aggressive business person and decided to utilize unconventional strategies to grow Walmart. Walmart utilized scales of economy and supply chain to bring the lowest price products to the US consumer. Walmart created giant stores where the consumer could enter knowing that he can purchase almost anything he needs in his home at the lowest price available in the market. Walmart also decided to grow first in rural areas rather than big cities thus establishing clear lead over other competitors by taking advantage as a first mover. Walmart became the largest American company at one point and Mr. Warren Buffet considers not investing in Walmart as one of his biggest mistakes.

10

INNOVATION AND ECONOMIES OF NATIONS

. . . .

D
uring the American civil war, factories in Europe suffered from lack of supply of cotton from America. They reached out to the traders in Bombay, India (now Mumbai) who could supply Indian cotton. Supply constraints increased cotton prices multiple times and these traders became super rich. A number of top industrial houses in India have their roots from those cotton trading days of 1860s. So, though the world was always connected, modern technology, telecommunications and globalization have changed the world economy in the last decade.

The term "macro" in macro-economics traditionally referred to a nation. Almost all theories of macro-economics are based on the cause and effect studies within the boundaries of a Nation. There are theories of the impact of demand and supply on the economic growth and prices. Similarly, there are theories of the impact of fiscal deficit and trade deficit on inflation. Almost all the time the object of the study is a Nation.

Globalization, however, bring the need to include "Globe" in the term "macro" of macro-economics, may be the correct term should be 'globo macro economics'.As the example of cotton trad-ing suggested, while global trade has been in existence for a long time, modern telecommunications has made it grow at an unprecedented pace. While it took months and years for factories to be shut down and moved abroad, the service sector jobs can now be moved in a few days. Non-uniform tax laws for corporations in different countries have made it difficult for outsiders to identify what part of a firm's profits are coming locally and what are coming from internationally.

While nations strived for self sufficiency for a long time, the modern concept of globalization stresses on the virtues of inter-dependency among nations. Perhaps, the current generation of human beings in the world is participating in an experiment of global economics, and the effects will be studied in the future. Only time will tell if globalization would be beneficial for most nations and people or it is another utopian concept. The older macro economics concepts are not enough to predict future in this new global system, it was highlighted by the fact that none of top economists was able to forecast the great recession of 2008-09 which caused worldwide impact.

World leaders have realized that there would be intense competition to the companies of their countries due to globalization and they have been urging their people to be more innovative. The nations that are dominant today in the world economy had realized the importance of innovation much earlier than those that are still developing.

Nations and Innovation:

For a long time, the Western economies have been blessed with great scientists whose fundamental research led to creation of wealth for the western world. Almost all the top 100 scientists listed (http://www.adherents.com/people/100_scientists.html) who shaped world history were in the western countries.

However, in the 1970s, Japanese companies realized that to grow their economy, they should utilize existing fundamental research and use innovation as the main source of developing new products. Japanese utilized this faster way to creation of wealth. Instead of relying on doing fundamental research which has long gestation period, Japanese started by taking the incremental approach to innovation. Later, with the growth of wealth, Japanese also invested in fundamental research and developed leading edge products using that research. Let us understand this by comparing innovation in US and Japan:

United States and Innovation:

United States, in particular has benefited the most from Fundamental research – mostly funded by government directly or indirectly.

US universities were a place of collaboration between the academia and the Industry and therefore investment in R&D brought innovation based on fundamental research. Accounting and Taxation rules encouraged spending on R&D in United States. This research was then used by the Industry to create new products and expand their businesses.

A mature and large sized Venture Capital industry in United States is also a result of government laws and tax benefits that allow and encourage risk-capital, that is investment in Venture Capital industry by the various funds like Pension funds, endowment funds etc. These entities are allowed to allocate a small percentage of their funds to the Venture Capital industry. These organizations trust venture capitalists to identify and invest in new technologies and innovative companies. There is a high risk of loss of capital in this new companies, but the upside potential for successful companies is also very high. To give an example, an investment of 300 K in hotmail.com by the venture capitalist returned him 80 million dollars in less than two years. Entities like Pension funds are also exempt from any Capital Gains tax.

Machines, Electricity, Railways, Airlines, cars, computers, tele-communications, new drugs and internet – almost everything came out from United States.

And with these came periods of economic booms. The boom of 1920s was caused by automobile and radio Industry, the boom of 1950s-1960s was caused by consumer goods or lifestyle goods like TVs, Dish washers, washing machines etc, the boom after mid 1980s was caused by the electronics and the personal computer Industry. The boom of 1990s was created by the growth of Personal Computers, Mid-sized computers, Software companies, the internet, telecom and computer services companies.

Thereafter, the period from 2004 to 2007 was called the period of web 2.0. During this period, the internet had reached majority of United States homes. Therefore social networking became popular and many companies like Google, Facebook, Linkedin etc started becoming popular. (Another important factor during this period was high consumer credit and very low interest rates in this short-growth period).

However, the interest rates in United States spiraled upwards from 2005 to 2008, thus breaking the capacity of consumers who had taken too much debt during the previous few years. Further, no fundamentally new technologies came out or became popular in United States (and the world in general) in 2000s. Together, these factors created a decline in the real economic growth.

Starting with early 2000s when conservative ideology became popular, another important change has been happening in United States. Most employees, who previously had lifelong permanent employment along with full post retirement pension benefits found that their employment in organizations is short term and is dependent on their need for short term and specific projects. Like other Americans, Scientists also find themselves in similar unsecure jobs and they also do not have guaranteed or defined pension benefits. These conditions are not conducive to free thinking and thinking outside the box. Scientists need to have free mind to come up with new innovative solutions. As an example, the Optical fiber, which has revolutionized the telecom industry worldwide was not developed in a planned project of any telecom company, but inside Corningware, a glass factory. The engineers in Corningware had ample freedom to experiment with new ideas and they came up with the Optical fibre.

Similarly, the internet were not conceived or developed as per a pre-defined project, but was created over a period of time by scientists who had the time and resources to experiment with creation of point to point networking between different types of computers. They further utilized the TCP protocol, which became a standard in 1980s to expand the network of computers.

The new economic environment would hurt fundamental research work in United States.

Japan and Innovation:

Japanese economy, on the other hand, grew based on an incremental approach to innovation. Japanese did not focus on doing fundamental research, but used existing technologies to produce better and more consumer centric products:

Japanese did not invent cars or the assembly line but produced optimum quality cars at affordable prices; Japanese did not create any breakthrough electronics but created more user friendly and higher quality electronic products based on existing set of research base.

At one point, Japanese economy became the 2nd largest economy (despite having a very small land area and a small population).

Japanese taught to the world that in order to do innovation and grow businesses, you do not necessarily need institutions of fundamental research (like American laboratories and universities). By using existing set of technologies and understanding the requirements of different customer segments, new desirable consumer products can be created.

Japanese knew that the key to innovation is not reaching the maximum comfort level or providing the most number of features, but to reach an optimum level.

Japanese cars were not the most comfortable cars; in fact these were less comfortable than the American cars due to their smaller space. Japanese cars were also not the best quality cars (these were considered inferior to the German cars), but had an optimum comfort and an optimum quality which the customer would be willing to pay for. Despite lacking any MBA programs in Japan for a long time, Japanese were able to understand the need of the consumer very carefully.

There are different approaches to fulfilling customer needs, even within the different car companies: While Toyota gives a choice of hundreds of customizations in its cars at the choice of the customer; Honda gives a choice of 3 to 4 versions in the same model (example LX, VX, V6) etc. Some customers prefer to have detailed customization done to the cars they purchase, others prefer not to do customization and prefer to choose from the company's pre-selected versions.

I would give a personal example here. In 1989, I traveled from India to Hong Kong for a vacation. Those days Japanese VCRs had just started becoming popular in India, and I bought a VCR for my family in India. When I opened the VCR box back in India, I was surprised that one of the few Instruction manuals was in Hindi, my native language. It occurred to me that Japanese knew that there was a high probability for this particular VCR to be reaching a North Indian home ! This was particularly remarkable as unlike these days when India is considered a high growth emerging economy, India had a small closed economy, there was no internet in India and very few foreign companies had permission to open business in India

In my later chapters, besides discussing the frameworks of doing innovation, I would also focus on what kind of innovation would the customers be willing to pay for.

Emerging Economies, Innovation and their Challenges:

Kiran Mazumdar-Shaw is the owner of billion-dollar BIOCON, a biotechnology company based in Bangalore, India. She learnt the concepts of large scale wine making processes due to her family being in this business. Later, when she learnt biotechnology, she realized that there is a need to create economies of scale for biotechnology products. She combined the knowledge of large scale manufacturing processes for Wines with the knowledge of production of Biotechnology products and created a solid-substrate fermentation processes. Ms Mazumdar-Shaw has taken this startup company to become one of the largest Biotechnology companies in the world in a short period.

The economies of countries like China and India have been growing rapidly for the last two decades, and there have been many innovations there. Due to lack of access to leading edge fundamental research, the innovations in these countries have been in the areas of services and processes, as explained by the success of BIOCON. Chinese companies have focused on manufacturing industries, creating cost-effective products. They have been able to manufacture products utilizing lesser amount of material or lower cost raw materials. One the other hand, Indian companies have focused on finding services where they can complete the work at a faster pace and utilizing workforce spread across different continents. Indian companies are able to complete software based projects in a more cost effective way and at a faster pace using what is known as the 'Global

Delivery method'. Due to the time zone difference of ten and a half hours, while it is night time in US, it is day time in India. Therefore, the software development work can be done almost non-stop on a 24 hours basis. Indian companies also have the advantage of a large base of English speaking population.

With the success of the emerging country corporations, these countries now have surplus cash funds. It is expected that these countries will be doing serious innovation which for long has been the turf of developed economies till now.

Emerging market products and quality:

Though products from emerging countries have become popular in the US market for most consumer goods, these products are not particularly known for very high quality. Instead, these are manufactured for the cost-conscious segment of the customers. Some of these products also use different standards for design and construction of various parts compared to the American products. With high inflation in emerging countries and strong pressure from western leaders about currency exchange rates, emerging countries would need to increase the prices of their products and that would be difficult unless they work on improving the quality of their products.

DISPOSABLE INCOME - A US
Economy Innovation:

As we have discussed that every economic boom in United States has been caused by the growth of new technologies and products. In the 1920s, we witnessed growth of automobile and radio industry; in the 1950s and 1960s, United States witnessed growth of consumer goods like TVs, Dish washers and Washing Machines; in mid-1980s, there was growth of electronics and personal computers; and in the 1990s, there was growth in internet and telecom based companies.

However, the demand for these new products was caused due to people in United States having high disposable incomes. Perhaps, high disposable income is itself the biggest innovation in the US economy. Disposable income is the amount of money which a person can spend from his income after spending on basic necessities like food, shelter and fuel. High disposable incomes create demand for new products and services. The disposable income increases either by increase in wage or reduction in the spending requirements for basic necessities.

The concept of high disposable income is one of the core concepts behind the growth of United States economy. The nation started with large natural resources (and later industrially produced goods) and a small population base. It was a challenge to create enough demand to enable the consumption of produced goods. The nation faced many severe recessions in the 19th century, before the great depression of last century. Therefore, while it suited other nations with small base of natural and produced resources and comparatively large population sizes, to pay low wages for the same work, high wages were suitable for the sustainable growth of the U.S. economy. High disposable income became the key reason that people from Europe and later from other countries immigrated to United States. An increase or decrease in disposable income gets reflected in the economy in the medium term.

One of the important reasons for the great recession of 2008-09 was because the disposable income of common people in United States had shrunk due to high interest rates (increased over a dozen time from 2004 to 2007), high gas prices (crossed $4 per gallon), high inflation, high home prices and stagnant wages. These factors resulted in people cutting down on discretionary spending and some people defaulting on their loan payments, which made the recession even more severe. Similarly, the economy came out of recession in 2009 due to interest rates going drastically down, home prices going down, gas prices going from $4 to $2 a gallon and inflation going down, thus increasing the disposable income of working people, despite the wages being still stagnant.

As production capacity of emerging markets has increased in the last few decades due to industrialization and transfer of knowledge due to information technology, the concept of high disposable income has now gone to the emerging countries from United States.

As I have discussed in the previous chapter "Consumer Psychology and the new Products", if an innovative product increases productivity by saving the consumer time, effort or cost in doing his work, it would create a demand at almost any time. On the other hand, if the innovative product is fulfilling a non-obvious or hidden need, the consumer would consider the cost of the new product and will make a decision based on his disposable income. Such products like a Microwave oven, a DVD player or an LCD TV became popular only in a small section of the consumers when they were launched.

In the 1980s, the Japanese focused on exporting their products – they ensured that their products which were made in Japan were sold for a cheaper price outside Japan than within Japan. Many times, Japanese people flew from Japan to Hong Kong to purchase Japanese products as these were way cheaper in Hong Kong.

Perhaps innovation and disposable income are inter-linked variables for the growth of US economy. While high disposable income creates demand for new products, innovation helps in creating new products to fulfill that demand. So unless US wants to have a an export-based economy, for a long term sustainable growth, United States would need to focus both on creating an eco-system for innovation within its borders as well as ensure that the consumers have high disposable income so that there is consistent demand for new products.

11

NATIONAL LAWS
AND INNOVATION

· ·

Intellectual Property Laws in Developing and Developed Nations:

In a store of Starbucks coffee chain in New York, I ordered a cup of coffee. As I picked up the paper cup containing coffee, I noticed a sleeve around the cup. It was made up of a cardboard and it protected my hand from the hot coffee cup. When I looked at it carefully it said "US Patent # 5, 205, 473 and 6863644".

(picture of the jacket with the US patent# is displayed below)

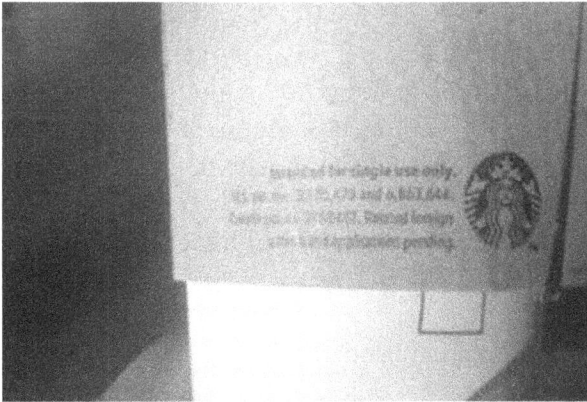

Though the product is simple, it is made up of a cardboard sheet and anybody can replicate it without much research. However, it is illegal in the US to replicate it. The United States government recognizes that somebody has applied his creativity to produce a useful product. That "someone" has not done it for charity or to alleviate human suffering, but to make money from his innovation. Unless that goal is protected, there would be no incentive for him or others who want to create new products.

Strong protection of intellectual property rights, fast decisions by courts and allowing victims to claim enormous amounts running into tens or hundreds of million dollars as damages has ensured that United States remains the center of the world for innovation.

I would contrast this with the situation in emerging countries, for example, India. Though there are intellectual property rights in India, enforcing the laws is generally difficult. Firstly, the police has not been well informed about the violation of the Intellectual Property rights. Till the late 1980s, Police in India considered copying software as a trivial crime. Software companies in the US then started utilizing a lobbying organization NASSCOM (National Association of Software and Services Companies) to educate the law enforcement authorities in India about the need to enforce intellectual property rights and why it would be helpful to the economy. NASSCOM was instrumental in getting conducted police raids at places doing software piracy. Dewang Mehta, the famous chief of Nasscom those days started organizing many seminars for senior law enforcement officers and later got the first toll-free phone in the country where he encouraged people to inform him of software piracy in the country. He also worked with local police officers to conduct raids on people doing software privacy.

In case of an intellectual property dispute, the court cases can take a very long time to make decisions. It is common in India, for court cases to take more than 10 years to get a decision just in the lower court. The losing party in the case would usually take the case to higher courts which would take another decade.

Another hindrance to getting justice for intellectual property disputes in India is due to the concept of Stamp Duty requirements of the court. If somebody wants to claim damages, he has to first pay stamp duty which is calculated as a percentage of the claim in advance.

As an example if somebody wants to claim $40,000 as damages, he has to first deposit $600 as a stamp duty in the court in advance in some states in India. Due to such laws and the fact that court cases can take decades, it is nearly impossible for people to rightfully claim any damages in case their Intellectual property is misused. As it is said, justice delayed is similar to justice denied.

Fundamental research and innovation, both contribute to producing new works useful to the consumers. United States laws have been most aggressively protecting both fundamental research as well as application of this research for new innovative products. After the advent of internet, many internet companies were also able to get their online business processes patented. However, what constitutes something that can be patented is not the same across the world. What can be patented in one country may not be patentable in another country. In order to give a uniform and level playing field to innovators across the world, there needs to be a uniform legal code for creating and enforcing of patents. The WTO has been working with countries for TRIPS (Trade related aspects of Intellectual property rights) agreement, which would enable a minimum common standard for safety of intellectual property rights across the world.

Outdated Laws hindering Innovation :

Till the early 1980s, most large corporations in United States were offering long term careers. Corporations expected employees to invest all their time in and out of office either performing their duties or thinking of supporting the organizations. That was when the organizations had a hierarchical structure. During those days, all employees were asked to sign an invention-disclosure agreement. This agreement required that any invention or innova-tion by the employee would belong to the organization. The employee would give all the rights and patents on his invention to the organization.

The law made sense in the last century, but in the 21st century, this law is outdated and a hindrance to the innovation based growth of US economy. Let me elaborate on this:

In the 1990s, HR departments started implementing the matrix style of organization structure. In this structure, an employee was expected to only master a narrow area of skill set and was responsible to serve many groups with that skill set. There was no time for the organization to train or groom an employee in this new structure, the employee was supposed to be productive from day one as otherwise he would become a bottleneck to projects of multiple groups. Many organizations did not even have plans of growing their employees into senior level roles on a routine basis. The employee would have no free time in this matrix environment to learn new skills or take additional roles. One impact of this structure was that employees became easily

Sanjeev Sharma

replaceable commodities due to their narrow skill sets and roles. After the mid-1990s, many leading organizations also changed their fixed-benefits retirement plans to fixed-contribution based plans. By the end of 1999, almost all organizations had washed their hands off from post-retirement needs of employees, besides the minimum contribution to their employees'401K plans.

Further, almost all CEOs had started getting stock options as part of their compensation. Since Stock options can be cashed only if the stock price is higher that the strike price, CEOs started focusing on short term earnings rather than long term growth of the organizations. And cost cutting by laying off employees became an easy tool in hands of CEOs to show profitability in the short term. Most employees in United States today are easily replaceable commodities used by organizations on a project and need basis and are asked to leave almost immediately after the project ends. Therefore, it is natural for many employees to think of starting their own companies in their spare time. Many of them would think of new innovative solutions and products. However, as the relationship between the employees and organizations are not long term, employees do not see any value in sharing their inventions with their organizations and they should not be forced to give up their rights on their inventions.

Large organizations have their own business agenda and many innovations by employees are not relevant to the strategy of the organization. These organizations therefore do not make the required efforts to commercialize the innovations by the employees. Research done in IBM Corporation on relational databases could have been used by IBM to create a Relational Database system on non mainframe based system, but it was used by Larry Ellison to start ORACLE, a database company based on UNIX and Windows operating systems. Oracle, now is one of the largest IT companies. Similarly, though Personal Computer was created by IBM, but IBM chose to outsource the operating system and the chip design to Microsoft and Intel. IBM had the capacity to create the operating system and chip for the personal computer but

214

developing these components was not a business priority of IBM at that time. Microsoft and Intel utilized this opportunity and are now very large corporations (Microsoft's Market Capitalization became bigger than IBM and the market value of Intel is around half that of IBM).

In these circumstances, due to invention-disclosure agreements which were started during the old days of long term employment system, ensure that these employees are neither able to patent/ protect their inventions nor commercialize these ideas into new businesses. As we have discussed before, innovations are important for the growth of a Nation's economy and therefore Innovations belong to the nation more than the individual or the company. Therefore, such outdated laws that discourage and slow the speed of innovations and inventions, need to be given a second look by the lawmakers.

IBM files the highest number of patents every year, submitted by its employees. IBM does not have the capacity to grow each of these patents into a commercial products. Many times, IBM is able to sell or license some of these patents to outside companies. The outside organizations utilize the technologies based on their need, but that may not be the best utilization of these technologies. Outside organizations lack the passion of the inventor to create an eco-system around the technology to make it a commercially successful product. The utilization of many technologies is not understood by outside organizations. Sometimes, it takes decades before the technology is commercialized.

Traditionally, 30 to 40% of net new jobs are added to US economy by small companies. As we discussed in the previous chapter, a large amount of money that was supposed to be allocated to the early stage ventures is now being utilized for other purposes. It has been found that only 4% of the Venture Capital investment is going to early stage companies in United States. The government has been contemplating supporting innovative companies by creating a national seed fund and it is important for the government to create an ecosystem to support new companies and remove any impediments to the formation of new companies.

Future of Innovation:

The increased access to information in a highly networked world would lead to a rapid generation of new products and services in the near future. Governments would need to remove barriers to innovation and encourage new entrepreneurs. While a large number of new products can now be created using the innovation frameworks described here, the skills to identify which of these innovations would be commercially successful would be important for businesses. Just like the science of statistics has been applied to do analytics work, similarly the science of consumer psychology would need to be applied to innovation frameworks to identify the non-obvious needs of consumers. Industry would also be rewarding people with talent to search relevant research work and apply it in the innovation work of organizations.

END NOTES

Chapter 1:

1. http://en.wikipedia.org/wiki/Glasses

2. *Dennis Ritchie: http://en.wikipedia.org/wiki/Dennis_Ritchie*

Chapter 2:

1. http://articles.timesofindia.indiatimes.com/2011-10-09/nri-achievers/30260109_1_computer-chip-photonic-computer-processors

2. http://www.npr.org/2011/09/07/140256967/shipping-container-inventor-transformed-world-trade

Chapter 3:

1. http://www.businessweek.com/magazine/content/10_28/b4186048358596.htm

Chapter 4:

1. http://www.washingtonpost.com/politics/postal-service-names-3700-post-offices-that-could-be-closed/2011/07/26/gIQARk3tbI_story.html

2. http://en.wikipedia.org/wiki/1-Click

3. http://en.wikipedia.org/wiki/Joseph_Schumpeter

Chapter 5:

1. http://www.idealab.com/press/pressreleasefinalapproved_version_for_ktk_launch_.pdf

2. http://www.slime.com/product/82/Tube-Sealant.html

3. http://en.wikipedia.org/wiki/Wankel_engine

4. From: http://gizmodo.com/299525/bomb-detector-powered-by-bee-tongue

5. http://en.wikipedia.org/wiki/Swimming_machine

6. www.endlesspools.com/

7. http://en.wikipedia.org/wiki/Claw_crane)

8. http://en.wikipedia.org/wiki/Cow_dung

Chapter 6:

1. http://www.time.com/time/magazine/article/0,9171,1893507,00.html

2. http://www.grameeninfo.org/index.php?option=com_content&task=view&id=28&Itemid=108

3. http://seekingalpha.com/article/317732-using-buffett-s-favorite-ratio-to-analyze-the-dow

4. http://en.wikipedia.org/wiki/Dutch_East_India_Company

5. http://en.wikipedia.org/wiki/Derivative_%28finance%29

6. http://en.wikipedia.org/wiki/Insurance

7. http://en.wikipedia.org/wiki/Watch

8. http://www.wired.com/gadgets/gadgetreviews/news/2008/07/atomicwatches_reviews

9. http://en.wikipedia.org/wiki/Partsearch_Technologies

10. http://www.dnforum.com/f17/diapers-com-sold-540-million-dollars-thread-437786.html

Chapter 7:

1. (http://en.wikipedia.org/wiki/Evaporative_cooling#Evaporative_cooling)

2. http://www.google.com/products/catalog?hl=en&client=firefox-a&hs=irp&rls=org.mozilla:en-US:official&channel=np&q=Dual+flush+toilet+tank&gs_upl=6877l8080l1l8336l6l5l0l0l0l4l735l1179l5l2-2.5-1.1l4l0&bav=on.2, or.r_gc.r_pw., cf.osb&biw=1024&bih=629&um=1&ie=UTF-8&tbm=shop&cid=18274880686722133671&sa=X&ei=dgDlTtj5E8rt0gG9nNzUBQ&ved=0CJQBEPICMAM

3. http://www.aptera.com/learn.php

4. http://www.eSolar.com

5. http://www.fastcompany.com/1786799/nissans-10-minute-car-charger-could-change-the-electric-vehicle-landscape?partner=gnews

6. http://www.thehindu.com/business/companies/article2230252.ece

7. http://dishworldiptv.com/

Chapter 8:

1. http://bits.blogs.nytimes.com/2009/02/02/venture-capital-returns-dip-below-zero/

2. http://www.khoslaventures.com/khosla/people_vk.html

3. http://www.msnbc.msn.com/id/21756222/ns/business-going_green/t/al-gore-joins-top-venture-capital-firm/

4. http://genxfinance.com/bootstrapping-your-start-up-business-with-little-or-no-money/

ABOUT THE AUTHOR:

. . . .

S anjeev Sharma is a New York based consultant with nearly twenty years of experience in finance, venture capital and technology roles in USA and India. He was one of the first managers in the early stages of National Stock exchange of India in mid 1990s. He provided leadership to many mission critical projects at IBM Corporation, USA and provided business and product development support to many early stage portfolio companies in the venture capital industry. He also taught finance to management students and has accurately predicted the movement of US economy and stock market for the last five years, at seekingalpha.com.

Sanjeev holds an MBA from Columbia Business School, New York and can be reached at **ciframeworks@yahoo.com.**